HEADLINE SERIES

No. 303   FOREIGN POLICY ASSOCIATION   Summer

Nuclear Proliferation:
The Post-Cold-War Challenge

by Ronald J. Bee

Cover Design: Ed Bohon

D1265344

$5.95

The Author

RONALD J. BEE, currently at the University of California Institute on Global Conflict and Cooperation in San Diego, was director of research at ACCESS: A Security Information Service based in Washington, D.C., from 1990 to 1992. He has written, taught and commentated extensively on international security issues.

The Foreign Policy Association

The Foreign Policy Association is a private, nonprofit, nonpartisan educational organization. Its purpose is to stimulate wider interest and more effective participation in, and greater understanding of, world affairs among American citizens. Among its activities is the continuous publication, dating from 1935, of the HEADLINE SERIES. The author is responsible for factual accuracy and for the views expressed. FPA itself takes no position on issues of U.S. foreign policy.

HEADLINE SERIES (ISSN 0017-8780) is published four times a year, Spring, Summer, Fall and Winter, by the Foreign Policy Association, Inc., 729 Seventh Ave., New York, N.Y. 10019. Chairman, Paul B. Ford; President, John Temple Swing; Editor in Chief, Nancy Hoepli-Phalon; Senior Editors, Ann R. Monjo and K.M. Rohan; Editorial Assistant, June Lee. Subscription rates, $20.00 for 4 issues; $35.00 for 8 issues; $50.00 for 12 issues. Single copy price $5.95; double issue $11.25. Discount 25% on 10 to 99 copies; 30% on 100 to 499; 35% on 500 and over. Payment must accompany all orders. Postage and handling: $2.50 for first copy; $.50 each additional copy. Second-class postage paid at New York, N.Y., and additional mailing offices. POSTMASTER: Send address changes to HEADLINE SERIES, Foreign Policy Association, 729 Seventh Ave., New York, N.Y. 10019. Copyright 1995 by Foreign Policy Association, Inc. Design by K.M. Rohan. Printed at Science Press, Ephrata, Pennsylvania. Summer 1993. Published February 1995.

Library of Congress Catalog Card No. 94-61086
ISBN 0-87124-160-9

The Dawn of
Nuclear Proliferation

Early in the morning of July 16, 1945, scientists and soldiers huddled in the sands of a New Mexico desert, peering nervously at the 100-foot-high steel tower, designated Point Zero. Nervously, because of the time, money and effort spent over three years in strict secrecy to build the 10,000-pound contraption, nicknamed Fat Man, now hanging awkwardly from that tower. Nervously, because many observers thought that what was about to happen at Alamogordo could very well serve to end the unprecedented bloodshed of World War II. And nervously, because some scientists present feared that the impending first test of an atomic bomb* might destroy the state of New Mexico, or ignite the atmosphere and obliterate the entire world.

At 5:10 a.m., Dr. J. Robert Oppenheimer, scientific director for the operation code-named Manhattan Project, clung

*See glossary, pp. 66–68.

to a post in the control center as his assistant began the countdown to zero hour. General Leslie R. Groves, military director of the project, noted, "As the remaining time was called from the loudspeaker, from the 10,000-yard control station there was complete silence." General Thomas F. Farrell, assistant to Groves, recalled, "Everyone in that room knew the awful potentialities of the thing that they thought was about to happen." Farrell added, "We were reaching into the unknown and we did not know what might come of it."

Upon detonation, the blast was visible for 180 miles in every direction. At a distance of 10 miles from Point Zero, the intensity of the light equaled 1,000 suns. Fat Man exploded with the force of some 17,000 tons of TNT, a form of dynamite that until then had been the most destructive explosive. Unlike TNT, however, the bomb released enough radiation to kill every living thing within a radius of two thirds of a mile.

This was the dawn of the nuclear age and the advent of nuclear proliferation. Before the first atomic bomb test, Manhattan Project scientists were uncertain whether such a bomb could be built and exploded; afterward, they not only knew that the principles of atomic fission* worked but also that they could start building these bombs for use against the Japanese.

In August 1945, the United States dropped atomic bombs on the Japanese cities of Hiroshima and Nagasaki (highly enriched uranium* was used in the Hiroshima bomb; plutonium,* in the Nagasaki bomb). The blast, heat and radiation effects caused so many deaths and such devastation that the Japanese surrendered several days after the attack on Nagasaki. Since that time, no other nuclear weapon has been used in wartime, and a major goal of U.S. foreign policy has been to prevent the further spread, or proliferation, of nuclear weapons to other countries.

At present, five nations admit to having nuclear arsenals: the United States (first test, 1945), Russia (as a successor to the Soviet Union, 1949), Britain (1952), France (1960) and

The cloud formed by a 1954 hydrogen bomb test seen at a distance of 50 miles from the detonation site.

the People's Republic of China—PRC (1964). Israel is widely thought to have an undeclared nuclear arsenal; India, which conducted a "peaceful" nuclear test in 1974, and Pakistan have admitted to possessing a nuclear capability but deny they have arsenals. South Africa revealed in March 1993 that it had developed six nuclear weapons, but it claims to have destroyed them in 1990. Iraq, North Korea, Iran, Libya and Taiwan are also suspected of harboring nuclear ambitions.

The New Post-Cold-War Challenge

Although the end of the cold war and the disintegration of the Soviet Union in 1991 reduced the threat of nuclear war between the two superpowers, the potential sale or transfer of former Soviet nuclear-weapons materials, technology

---

CTBT: comprehensive test-ban treaty
IAEA: International Atomic Energy Agency
NPT: Treaty on the Non-Proliferation of Nuclear Weapons

and know-how remains a real concern. Beside the possibility of "nuclear yard sales," certain newly independent republics may have reasons for keeping a nuclear arsenal. For example, some Ukrainian leaders have voiced a residual interest in possessing nuclear arms to deter possible Russian ambitions.

In addition to the nuclear uncertainties created by the Soviet breakup, two glaring proliferation problems—Iraq and North Korea—have held center stage in the post-cold-war era. Iraq sought to develop nuclear weapons secretly despite being a party to the 1968 Treaty on the Non-Proliferation of Nuclear Weapons (NPT),* which expressly forbids it to seek a nuclear-weapons capability. After Iraq invaded Kuwait in 1990, concerns mounted about Iraqi nuclear activities. On April 3, 1991, the United Nations Security Council passed Resolution 687, which required the dismantling of Iraq's nuclear-weapons program. After repeated violations of inspection agreements, UN coalition forces led by the United States attacked suspected Iraqi nuclear facilities during and after Operation Desert Storm. While most experts believe the UN-mandated destruction of Iraq's nuclear facilities neutralized the Iraqi program for the short-term, it still poses a significant long-term threat. On September 23, 1993, President Bill Clinton sent a letter to Congress on Iraqi compliance with UN Security Council resolutions that said, "Saddam Hussein is committed to rebuilding his WMD* [weapons of mass destruction] capability, especially nuclear weapons...."

North Korea, an NPT signatory, caused a second post-cold-war nuclear crisis in 1994 that could embroil Northeast Asia in armed conflict. Most experts contend that what happens in North Korea will have a great impact on the future of nuclear nonproliferation. If North Korea (a Communist nation increasingly isolated in the post-cold-war world) produces a bomb, many worry that South Korea and Japan may consider developing their own nuclear options. At issue was North Korea's refusal to permit inspections of suspected nuclear sites, its threat to withdraw from the NPT, its unsupervised removal from a reactor of nuclear fuel that could be diverted to producing nuclear weapons, and its withdrawal from the International Atomic Energy Agency (IAEA).*

By June 1994, the United States, allied with South Korea, sought UN economic sanctions against North Korea; North Korea, in turn, replied that it would consider the imposition of sanctions as an act of war. South Korea mobilized over a million army reservists as a precaution, and the IAEA cut off technical aid to North Korea on June 10, 1994. North Korea withdrew from the agency three days later. Moreover, President Clinton warned that if North Korea attacked South Korea with nuclear weapons, it "would be the end of their country." A last-ditch personal diplomatic effort by former President Jimmy Carter in June may have averted war on the Korean peninsula. However, it took months of negotiations between the United States and North Korea to agree to a solution for outstanding nuclear issues. Optimists believe the

Tom Gibb, *Altoona Mirror*

agreement reached in October, calling for over $4 billion in energy aid to North Korea over the next 10 years in exchange for commitments to freeze and gradually dismantle its nuclear-weapons program, will successfully eliminate North Korea's nuclear ambitions. Skeptics, however, hold that there is no foolproof guarantee that North Korea will not use its production of plutonium to fabricate nuclear weapons.

Both the Iraqi and North Korean scenarios highlight a new post-cold-war imperative: the need to enforce international nonproliferation commitments while seeking ways to defuse tensions that could prompt regional arms races and conflicts. On September 27, 1993, speaking before the UN, President Clinton warned of the threat that proliferation poses to the interests of democracies everywhere:

> One of our most urgent priorities must be attacking the proliferation of weapons of mass destruction whether they are nuclear, chemical or biological, and the ballistic missiles that can rain them down on populations hundreds of miles away.... If we do not stem the proliferation of the world's deadliest weapons, no democracy can feel secure.

Dr. William J. Perry, U.S. secretary of defense, has further underscored the dangers: "I know of no problem with which the Department of Defense will be confronted more important than the problem of the proliferation of weapons of mass destruction." At least 20 countries, according to Perry, now have or are seeking to develop nuclear, chemical and/ or biological weapons and the means to deliver them.

Clearly these are not the only weapons to have wrought devastation and caused concern in this century. The overwhelming majority of deaths in World Wars I and II were caused by conventional weapons. As technology has improved weaponry and as weaponry has become deadlier, governments have felt compelled to build new weapons to keep up with or ahead of their adversaries.

What motivates nations to build and maintain nuclear arsenals in the first place? What historical, psychological and technological factors are at play? What strategies have been used to stop the spread of nuclear weapons? How relevant do they remain in the post-cold-war world? Which nations and regions represent the current proliferation hot spots? What are U.S. policy options for controlling nuclear proliferation?

Comprehending the fears generated by two world wars is essential for understanding why U.S. scientists strove to build the first atomic bomb and why leaders decided to use it. Fear subsequently played a crucial role in postwar nuclear proliferation and motivates today's nuclear aspirants. Nuclear weapons are so destructive that it is almost inconceivable that anyone would use them; yet nations maintain nuclear arsenals largely because they are afraid their rivals might use, or threaten to use, these weapons against them.

McGeorge Bundy, former national security adviser (1961–66) to Presidents John F. Kennedy and Lyndon B. Johnson, has also concluded that fear is primarily responsible for the proliferation of nuclear weapons:

> When we review the record, looking at the motives for the decisions of major governments, we find that…the dominant theme, beginning with Franklin Roosevelt in 1941, is fear—if we don't get it first, he [Hitler] may….[Roosevelt] got it so we must—Stalin in 1945; they are doing it, so must we—Britain and France; they have done it, and we will—Mao….Less fearful motives do operate: we will win; we will catch up; we will be great; we will even, perhaps, be safe. But fear dominates.

Three Nuclear Races

Nuclear proliferation stems from three different, but related, nuclear races. The first, involving the United States, Britain and Nazi Germany, began during World War II and ended at Hiroshima and Nagasaki. The second, between the United States and the Soviet Union, began at the end of World War II and resulted in the building of enormous nuclear arsenals by both superpowers and the creation of smaller stockpiles by Britain, France and China. The third is an ongoing contest between the spread of nuclear weapons and the prevention of nuclear war. This last race really began during the cold war, and it faces new hurdles in the post-cold-war era.

Race No. 1: Against the Nazis

In 1933, Albert Einstein, the famous physicist, emigrated to the United States, driven by the swelling tide of anti-Semitism in Germany. (Between 1933 and 1941 some 100 physicists left Germany for similar reasons.) Einstein and other refugee scientists came to fear that if Adolf Hitler, Germany's aggressive chancellor, were the first to develop an atomic bomb, he would use it to dominate the world. On the scientific front, German chemists Otto Hahn and Fritz Strassmann discovered uranium fission in 1938, when the world teetered on the edge of war and when German science was being tapped for military purposes. The German war department set up a secret atomic-bomb project, code-named The Uranium Society, that employed prominent German scientists.

After the German invasion of Poland in 1939, Einstein wrote President Franklin D. Roosevelt (1933–45) to alert him to the recent discoveries in atomic physics, the German bomb project and the destructive potential of an atomic bomb. The letter also urged support for U.S. atomic research as a prudent countermeasure. Since the United States still remained technically neutral, and the war remained far from home, Roosevelt committed only modest initial support for an advisory committee on uranium. Two years would pass before serious American work began on building a bomb.

On December 7, 1941, Japanese torpedo planes attacked the U.S. Pacific Fleet at Pearl Harbor, Hawaii, without warning. The United States declared war on Japan the following day. Four days after the attack on Pearl Harbor, Germany declared war on the United States. Now that America was at war with both Germany and Japan, more attention was paid to German nuclear research, and work began in earnest on the Manhattan Project. Germany, as it turned out, did not make serious progress toward producing nuclear weapons. It was, however, too late; the fears driving the first nuclear race had already begun to fuel a second competition.

Race No. 2: Between the Superpowers

One of the first efforts to stop nuclear proliferation took place before the original atomic bomb was tested at Alamogordo. Germany had surrendered in May 1945 and attention had turned to ending the war in the Pacific. On June 11, 1945, a committee of Manhattan Project scientists led by James Franck sent a secret report to U.S. Secretary of War Henry L. Stimson that argued against dropping atomic bombs on Japan. The Franck report also proposed revealing the U.S. atomic bomb project to the world in general, and the Soviets in particular, to quell the fears that might lead to a postwar nuclear arms race.

In the midst of mounting casualties, however, the overriding concern of U.S. leaders was to end the war as soon as possible. Isidor Rabi, a Manhattan Project scientist, noted, "And what would President Harry S. Truman [1945–53] say to the American people afterward? How could he explain to them that he had had a weapon to stop the war, but had been afraid to use it because it employed principles of physics that hadn't been used in wartime before?" Atomic bombs were dropped on Hiroshima and Nagasaki, and World War II ended.

As Europe and Japan lay in ruins, the postwar power struggle between the United States and the U.S.S.R. took center stage. The fact that the United States had a nuclear monopoly spurred the Soviets to develop their own capability. They conducted their first nuclear test in 1949. Despite high-fatality surrogate wars in Korea and Vietnam, actual hostilities never broke out between the United States and the Soviet Union. However, each side built bigger and larger numbers of nuclear weapons to deter attack or blackmail.

Some experts have argued that nuclear deterrence, as extensive and expensive as it became, served to preserve the peace for almost 50 years. Others, however, assert that peace was preserved in spite of—and not because of—this nuclear war of nerves. A fair number believe that a deterrent role could have been played by arsenals 100 times smaller than existing stockpiles. By 1967, the U.S. stockpile peaked at more than 32,000 nuclear warheads; the Soviet stockpile numbered 45,000 by the mid-1980s.

Bombs grew not only in numbers but also in destructive

potential. Hydrogen bombs* (H-bombs, or thermonuclear bombs) were developed by compressing lightweight atomic nuclei into a nucleus of heavier mass that creates temperatures high enough to ignite a rare heavy form of hydrogen known as deuterium. When temperatures reach 100 million degrees centigrade, the deuterium nuclei react in a way similar to what happens in the sun, a thermonuclear process called fusion.* Whereas the Hiroshima bomb employed fission, which splits nuclei, fusion joins, or fuses, them together.

Both fission and fusion release energy, but a fusion, or hydrogen, bomb can explode with at least a thousand times the force of fission bombs. The power of the first fission weapon tested in New Mexico was measured in kilotons, or thousands of tons, of TNT; hydrogen bombs are measured in terms of megatons, or millions of tons, of TNT. On November 1, 1952, the United States tested the first hydrogen bomb on the island of Elugelab, part of the Eniwetok atoll in the Pacific Ocean. Elugelab virtually disappeared, the bomb's mushroom cloud spread over 100 miles, and a 17-story building could have fitted in the mile-long crater it left in the ocean floor. The bomb's destructive power was measured at 12 megatons, nearly 600 times that of the Hiroshima bomb.

Not to be outdone, four years after testing their first fission weapon, the Soviets exploded their first hydrogen bomb on August 12, 1953. The U.S.S.R. went on to conduct the world's largest test—a 58-megaton hydrogen bomb that produced the most powerful explosion in history—in October 1961.

In a world threatened by hydrogen bombs, the word deterrence took on a new meaning. The term derives from the Latin word *deterrere,* which means "to frighten away from." Weapons with nuclear, let alone thermonuclear, power are fearful enough in themselves. But as McGeorge Bundy has reminded us, "fear of the bomb has always been less powerful than fear of the *adversary's* bomb....The weapons each side has sought have been those its government found necessary in the light of what others had done or might do." This proved true not only for the United States and the Soviet Union, but also for the three other nations—Britain, France and China—that decided to go nuclear in the wake of the superpower competition.

Britain's nuclear-weapons program, code-named Tube Alloys, began before British scientists joined the Manhattan Project in 1942. After the war, Britain pursued an independent course. In his book, *Britain and Nuclear Weapons,* Lawrence Freedman explains, "The postwar British program was determined by the assumption that a major power had little choice but to develop the most modern weapons available, and by the irritating fact that the Americans ended the postwar partnership in atomic research somewhat abruptly....It was felt that the only option was to go it alone and become a self-sufficient nuclear power." Britain exploded its first atomic bomb at Monte Bello, Australia, on October 3, 1952; it tested its first hydrogen bomb in May 1957. Britain's nuclear stockpile peaked in 1969 at 410 warheads.

France, driven by its history, nationalism and passion for independence, began seriously developing its own nuclear deterrent in 1954. Later, in his memoirs, President Charles de Gaulle described a letter he wrote to U.S. President Dwight D. Eisenhower (1953–61) explaining the rationale for an independent French *force de frappe:* "France has not forgotten what she owes to American help. But neither has she forgotten that during the first World War, that help came only after three long years of struggle which nearly proved mortal for her, and that during the second she had already been crushed before you intervened." The first French atomic test took place in the Sahara desert on February 17, 1960; France tested its first hydrogen bomb in August 1968. France reached its peak stockpile with 538 warheads in 1991.

The Chinese nuclear-weapons program began under PRC Chairman Mao Zedong in 1955 during an ongoing crisis with Taiwan and the United States over the two tiny island groups of Quemoy and Matsu. One year later Mao addressed party leaders on his reasons: "If we are not to be bullied in the present-day world, we cannot do without the bomb." Mao's commitment to revolution also reflected a credo that China must escape from generations of humiliation by stronger states. In seeking the bomb, he sought prestige and influence in international affairs commensurate with China's huge population and a counterforce to increasing Soviet and U.S. military strength. The first Chinese atomic test took place on October 16, 1964; China tested its first thermonuclear weapon in June 1967 and reached its present peak stockpile of 450 weapons in 1992.

An important lesson of the cold war for the post-cold-war world is that no country is likely to give up its nuclear weapons (or nuclear ambitions) while potential enemies continue to build, maintain or seek to establish nuclear arsenals. Looking at most of the current real or potential nuclear hot spots in the world—North Korea, India, Pakistan, Israel, Iraq, Iran, Ukraine and Russia—this lesson is as valid today as it was in the 1940s for the United States and the Soviet Union, or in the 1950s and 1960s for Britain, France and China.

Race No. 3: Against Nuclear Proliferation

As the ruins of World War II still smoldered, enthusiasm developed for the UN, an international organization founded in 1945 "to save succeeding generations from the scourge of war...." After the war, the United States tried to place nuclear weapons under UN authority. On June 14, 1946, Bernard M. Baruch, the U.S. representative to the UN Atomic Energy Commission, proposed the establishment of a permanent international authority to control, inspect and license all atomic reactors and materials to ensure their use for peaceful purposes only. Known as the Baruch Plan, it called for destroying all U.S. atomic bombs when international controls, including provisions to punish violators, were agreed upon. "If we fail," Baruch pleaded, "we have damned every man to be the slave of fear."

© Carnegie Endowment for International Peace

N. Korea

China

India

Pakistan

Russia

Kazakhstan

Israel

Iran

Iraq

Romania

Ukraine

Belarus

South Africa

Libya

Algeria

Britain

France

Brazil

Argentina

United States

Global Spread of Nuclear Weapons: 1995

DECLARED NUCLEAR-WEAPONS STATES: Britain, China, France, Russia, United States. All have declared their nuclear status and are recognized under the NPT as nuclear-weapons states because each detonated first nuclear tests prior to January 1, 1967.

NEWLY INDEPENDENT STATES WITH NUCLEAR WEAPONS ON TERRITORY: Belarus, Kazakhstan, Ukraine. All have joined NPT as nonnuclear-weapons states and will place all of their nuclear activities under IAEA inspection (excluding nuclear weapons still on their territory); all are transferring nuclear weapons to Russia; none is able to use remaining nuclear weapons independent of central command in Russia.

UNDECLARED NUCLEAR-WEAPONS STATES: India, Israel, Pakistan. All are able to deploy nuclear weapons rapidly, but have not acknowledged possessing them. None is party to the NPT. Israeli arsenal probably 100+ devices; Indian arsenal probably 60+; Pakistani arsenal probably 15–25.

RECENT RENUNCIATIONS: Algeria, Argentina, Brazil, Iraq, Romania, South Africa. Countries that were known or suspected to have secret nuclear-weapons programs in the past, but recently abandoned these goals by opening their nuclear facilities to international and/or regional inspection agencies, joining the NPT, and/or by terminating all research on nuclear arms. South Africa dismantled its program in the early 1990s and signed the NPT in 1991; the IAEA has verified complete dismantle- ment of all nuclear devices. Argentina and Brazil have both signed and ratified the Treaty of Tlatelolco and agreed to implement a system of comprehensive IAEA and bilateral inspections; in early 1995 Argentina took all the constitutional steps necessary to accede to the NPT. Algeria acceded to the NPT in January 1995.

ACTIVE/SUSPECTED NUCLEAR-WEAPONS PROGRAMS: Iran, Libya, North Korea. Nuclear-weapons ambitions are currently checked by international controls and technological constraints. Although the governments of these nations have officially "renounced" nuclear-weapons acquisition, they are believed to be actively interested in developing nuclear devices. North Korea is closest; recently agreed to freeze and ultimately dismantle its nuclear-weapons program under the October 1994 U.S.– North Korean agreement; may have separated enough weapons-grade material for a nuclear device. Iran is thought to be eight years from having nuclear weapons, but could accelerate program if nuclear assets leak from former Soviet Union. Libya has extremely limited nuclear infrastructure.

ABSTAINING COUNTRIES: Australia, Austria, Belgium, Canada, the Czech Republic, Denmark, Finland, Germany, Hungary, Ireland, Italy, Japan, Netherlands, Norway, Poland, Slovakia, South Korea and Spain. All are industrialized nations that have the technical capacity but not the political desire to develop nuclear weapons. Almost all of these nations operate nuclear reactors that are under IAEA inspection, and several have stocks of weapons-grade nuclear material, also under IAEA monitoring.

Five days later, a young Soviet diplomat, Andrei A. Gromyko, objected to Baruch's initiative. Gromyko did not want his country "invaded" by international inspectors, and he insisted that inspections be subject to Soviet veto. To this day, "verification procedures," that is, measures confirming an agreement has been kept, remain at the heart of the nuclear proliferation issue. The Soviets, then hard at work on their own bomb and worried about the American nuclear monopoly, stonewalled.

While the Baruch Plan never fully materialized, its principles and ideas resurfaced in December 1953 when President Eisenhower proposed an atoms-for-peace plan to the UN General Assembly. "To shake off the inertia imposed by fear," Eisenhower proposed establishing an "atomic energy agency...to devise methods whereby the fissionable material would be allocated to serve the peaceful pursuits of mankind." The 1957 Atoms-for-Peace Treaty, an implementation of Eisenhower's 1953 proposal, provided for the sharing of fissionable materials through the International Atomic Energy Agency (IAEA), based in Vienna, Austria. The goal of the IAEA was to "seek to accelerate and enlarge the contribution of atomic energy to peace, health and prosperity throughout the world" and to prevent the misuse of nuclear technology and materials for armaments.

The Baruch Plan, the Atoms-for-Peace Treaty and the founding of the IAEA represented the beginnings of what today is called the nuclear nonproliferation regime.* The Soviet erection of the Berlin Wall in 1961 and the Russian emplacement of nuclear missiles in Cuba in 1962 acted as catalysts in forming that regime. In both cases, the world came close to nuclear war, and in stepping back from the nuclear abyss, the United States and the Soviet Union realized that the third nuclear race, the race to prevent nuclear proliferation, merited closer attention.

The Nonproliferation Regime

After the Cuban missile crisis, President Kennedy and Soviet Premier Nikita S. Khrushchev realized they had a common interest in reducing the possibility of accidental nuclear war. Moreover, they began working in earnest on a treaty to stem the spread of nuclear weapons that also risked provoking a nuclear war. While Kennedy, assassinated on November 22, 1963, did not live to see the results, President Johnson vowed to follow the same policies. Among his accomplishments, Johnson signed the 1968 Treaty on the Non-Proliferation of Nuclear Weapons, which entered into force in March 1970. The NPT sought—and seeks—to make nuclear war less likely by preventing the spread of nuclear weapons to other countries.

The Nonproliferation Treaty

This treaty is the centerpiece of international efforts to curb the spread of nuclear weapons. The nonproliferation regime focuses on supply-side, or "denial," strategies that are implemented by an array of institutions and policies. Although it has not frozen the membership of the nuclear club, the regime has restrained countries with nuclear ambitions and reinforced an almost universal consensus against the further spread of nuclear weapons.

Since 1970, the NPT has become the most widely adhered to arms-control agreement in history. In January 1995, there were 170 signatories to the NPT. The NPT sought to freeze the number of nuclear-weapons states at five, and as of 1992, when France and China signed on, all five declared-nuclear-weapons states had become parties to the treaty. In signing the treaty, nuclear-weapons states pledge not to help non-nuclear-weapons states get the bomb and to facilitate "the fullest possible exchange of equipment, materials and scientific and technological information for the peaceful uses of nuclear energy." (Article IV) Nuclear-weapons states also promise to "pursue negotiations in good faith on effective measures relating to cessation of the nuclear arms race at an early date and to nuclear disarmament...." (Article VI)

Nonnuclear-weapons states, in signing the NPT, agree not to receive or manufacture nuclear weapons, to accept IAEA "safeguards,"* a system of accounting and monitoring of nuclear materials, and to declare and submit all nuclear materials they own to regular inspections. This is done to verify that nuclear materials have not been diverted from peaceful uses, for example, to the manufacture of nuclear weapons. (Article III) A working principle behind the NPT is that the positive incentive of access to civilian nuclear technology must be linked with the verification requirements of IAEA safeguards.

Since 1970, NPT members have held four review conferences, one every five years as required by the treaty. (Article VIII) The fifth and most important conference will convene in April 1995 in New York City, when members will "decide whether the treaty shall continue in force indefinitely, or shall be extended for an additional fixed period or periods." (Article X) The United States, Japan, Germany and Russia,

NPT: A Ready Reference

(summary of major articles)

ARTICLE I Nuclear-weapons states pledge not to transfer nuclear explosive devices or the means to produce them to nonweapons states.

ARTICLE II Nonweapons states pledge not to receive nuclear explosive devices or attempt to acquire them.

ARTICLE III Nonweapons states agree to IAEA safeguards— inspection of all nuclear activities and accounting for all nuclear materials.

ARTICLE IV Materials for the production of nuclear energy are excluded from the ban; parties are entitled—and can receive assistance—to use nuclear energy for peaceful purposes.

ARTICLE V The potential benefits of "peaceful nuclear explosions" conducted by weapons states will be made available on a nondiscriminatory basis.

ARTICLE VI The parties to the treaty, particularly the nuclear-weapons states, pledge to work toward "cessation of the nuclear arms race" and universal nuclear disarmament.

ARTICLE VII Regional associations have the right to declare their territories nuclear-free zones.

ARTICLE VIII Any party may propose an amendment to the treaty. When one third of the parties request it, a conference of all parties must be called for the purpose of considering the amendment. The treaty will be amended if a majority, including all weapons states party to the treaty (Britain, China, France, Russia and the United States), agree. Treaty-review conferences will be held every five years for twenty-five years.

ARTICLE IX A nuclear-weapons state is one which has manufactured and exploded a nuclear device prior to January 1, 1967.

ARTICLE X Parties may withdraw from the treaty on three-months notice if they deem their supreme interests to be jeopardized. A 1995 conference will determine whether the treaty shall continue in force indefinitely or be extended for an additional fixed period or periods.

to name a few, have proposed an unlimited extension of the NPT, while other countries have proposed extending it for periods ranging from five to twenty-five years. The initial duration of the treaty is 25 years, so a decision on its extension—whether for a fixed or indefinite period—must be made in 1995 by a majority vote of the NPT's membership.

International Atomic Energy Agency Safeguards

The International Atomic Energy Agency is a key component of the nuclear nonproliferation regime. Established on July 29, 1957, the IAEA is affiliated with the UN, but is autonomous. The agency plays two roles: one as a facilitator for transferring peaceful nuclear technology to developing nations, and the other as the primary organization for verifying compliance with the NPT. This dual role enables the IAEA to provide both positive and negative incentives for achieving nonproliferation objectives. The link between these two goals is often referred to as the nuclear bargain.

The NPT mandates that all nonnuclear-weapons states must negotiate IAEA safeguards agreements. The IAEA drafted a model NPT-type safeguards agreement and many nonnuclear states negotiated pacts based on it. Eventually, the United States, Britain and the U.S.S.R. opened all their civilian nuclear reactors to inspection, based on similar guidelines. France and China opened some, not all. All five excluded military-related facilities.

Not all members of the IAEA are parties to the NPT. Among the nonparties are India and Pakistan, which allow the IAEA to inspect some, but not all, of their nuclear facilities; both have negotiated non-NPT-type safeguards agreements. Two others, Argentina and Brazil, now have full-scope IAEA safeguards on all their nuclear activities.

The IAEA administrative structure resembles that of the UN. A General Conference includes all members (by January 1995, the agency had 122 members) and meets annually. A Board of Governors is comprised of 35 members: 9 are advanced nuclear nations and are permanent members; the rest serve one-year terms. The Board of Governors is the principal policymaking organ. The chief policymaking official is the director general, currently Dr. Hans Blix, a former Swedish foreign minister, who directs the secretariat, the administrative arm of the agency.

For a number of years, especially in the wake of revelations about the Iraqi nuclear program, many have criticized the adequacy of the IAEA safeguards system. Under current expectations, the IAEA's role should go from that of an international nuclear- materials auditor to an international police agency capable of uncovering, investigating and preventing the spread of nuclear weapons. A number of proposals have been advanced to strengthen the safeguards system: reform IAEA practices and procedures to improve the transparency of nuclear activities; adopt better definitions and more precise accounting methods for nuclear materials; reinvigorate the IAEA's authority to request and conduct special inspections; increase the IAEA's resources commensurate with its expanding mission; and bolster IAEA intelligence-gathering capabilities.

▶ *Increasing transparency:* The IAEA has already encouraged greater transparency in worldwide nuclear activities, in large part due to the lessons learned from Iraq and from North Korea's long delay in implementing its safeguards agreement. Before nuclear material is introduced, member states must provide nuclear-facility design information. Another suggestion has been to require countries to place a wider range of nuclear equipment, facilities and materials under safeguards. For example, in Iraq, large quantities of natural uranium and uranium oxide (sometimes called yellow-cake) were not under IAEA safeguards and were diverted for use in Iraq's nuclear-weapons program. Furthermore, the IAEA has proposed establishing an international register for all nuclear transfers, including dual-use technologies (that can be used for either civilian or military purposes).

▶ *Refining definitions and accounting methods:* Many experts believe that the IAEA's definition of the amounts of uranium

and plutonium needed to build a bomb is too high. (The current definition depicts 25 kilograms [55 lbs.] of highly enriched uranium or 8 kilograms [17.6 lbs.] of plutonium as a "significant quantity.") Smaller quantities, they say, such as 5 kilograms of plutonium or less, can build an effective nuclear bomb. Moreover, "material unaccounted for" in large nuclear facilities can exceed the amount needed to build nuclear weapons. New measurement technologies and better working definitions, it is argued, would close a loophole in the safeguards system and make it more difficult to divert weapons-grade material to build a bomb.

▶ *Conducting short-notice and special inspections:* While the IAEA has the authority to inspect undeclared nuclear sites, it did not exercise this right until the end of the cold war. Since 1991, inspections carried out in Iraq under a UN Security Council mandate have provided an example for the IAEA to follow in North Korea. Most experts contend that the IAEA must be more assertive in conducting such "challenge inspections" in order to remain a viable nuclear watchdog. Furthermore, in the past, inspections were arranged well in advance with member states, and inspectors could be denied access. Shorter notice of inspections would reduce the likelihood of states successfully hiding their nuclear activities. Inspectors could also be provided with pre-approved visas to prevent delays.

▶ *Augmenting IAEA resources:* Hiring more inspectors, conducting additional inspections and using new safeguards technologies require increased resources. New IAEA responsibilities include the denuclearization of Iraq, inspections of Argentine, Brazilian and South African nuclear facilities, and trying to cope with the nuclear environmental hazards in Eastern Europe and the former Soviet Union. Moreover, many have suggested that the IAEA take the lead in safeguarding the fissile materials from dismantled American and Russian nuclear warheads and participate in monitoring a global fissile-materials-cutoff regime. The IAEA operates with an annual budget of slightly more than $200 million, with $60 million allocated for safeguards. Despite expanded duties, the budget has been frozen for eight years.

▶ *Sharpening intelligence-gathering:* Good intelligence is key to the IAEA's doing its job well. Accurate intelligence is also important for building consensus among the IAEA Board of Governors and the UN Security Council when they deliberate action against a member state that is not complying with its NPT obligations. The IAEA was able to conduct effective inspections in Iraq because of intelligence provided by member states, in particular the United States. Similarly, member states shared intelligence on North Korea. Comparable co-operation may not always be forthcoming: governments are often reluctant to divulge their sources or the technologies they use to gather information for fear they may one day be used against them.

Other Elements of the Regime

● *Arms-control treaties addressing 'horizontal' proliferation:* Two other treaties complement the NPT in stemming horizontal proliferation, that is, the spread of nuclear weapons to countries beyond those who have them now: the Treaty for the

Prohibition of Nuclear Weapons in Latin America (also known as the Treaty of Tlatelolco) and the South Pacific Nuclear-Free Zone Treaty (also known as the Treaty of Rarotonga). The Treaty of Tlatelolco (1968) calls for the establishment of a nuclear-weapons-free zone covering Central and South America, including territories held in the region by nuclear-weapons states. The treaty requires parties to accept full-scope safeguards and prohibits nuclear-weapons states from using or threatening to use nuclear weapons in the region. Argentina and Brazil, after a long delay, finally ratified the treaty in 1994. The remaining holdout is Cuba.

The Treaty of Rarotonga (1986) prohibits the manufacture or acquisition of nuclear weapons by states in the South Pacific region and bans the emplacement of nuclear weapons there by nuclear-weapons states. Members of the Treaty of Rarotonga also have inspection agreements with the IAEA. Along with the Treaty of Tlatelolco, this treaty indirectly supports the NPT and reinforces the international consensus against the spread of nuclear weapons. While France agreed to a moratorium on nuclear testing at its site in French Polynesia, neither France nor the United States has signed the Treaty of Rarotonga. America's main argument for not signing is that the treaty would set a bad precedent for other regions where the United States may still need to maintain a nuclear deterrent, such as nuclear-armed submarines or intercontinental ballistic missiles. Legislation introduced in the 103d Congress, however, urged President Clinton to sign the treaty.

● *Arms-control treaties addressing 'vertical' proliferation:* Arms-control agreements also contribute to the nonproliferation regime by stemming vertical proliferation, that is, by controlling or reducing existing nuclear stockpiles. When nuclear powers conclude treaties such as the Limited Test Ban Treaty (LTBT, 1963), the Antiballistic Missile Treaty* (ABM, 1972), Strategic Arms Limitation Talks* (SALT I, 1972), the Threshold Test Ban Treaty (TTBT, 1974), the Peaceful Nuclear Explosions Treaty (PNE, 1976), the Intermediate

Nuclear Force Treaty* (INF, 1987), the Strategic Arms Reduction Treaty* (Start I, 1991) and (Start II, 1993), they not only can advance their own national interests but also the goals of vertical nonproliferation. Reducing nuclear arsenals can also serve to fulfill the pledge in Article VI of the NPT to "pursue negotiations in good faith on effective measures relating to cessation of the nuclear arms race at an early date."

● *The Zangger Committee:* In an effort to forge agreement among NPT members on what exports needed safeguards, the Zangger Committee, named after its first chairman, Claude Zangger of Switzerland, was formed in the early 1970s. The committee keeps an up-to-date list of materials and equipment "especially designed or prepared" for nuclear-nonweapons use—including such things as reactor components, reactors and certain nuclear materials such as heavy water—that could also be used for military purposes and are thus subject to IAEA safeguards. The Zangger "trigger list" also defines the technology and the criteria for determining what can or cannot be transferred to nonweapons states of the NPT under Article III.

● *The Nuclear Suppliers Group (NSG):* After the Indian nuclear test in 1974, more-restrictive nuclear-export guidelines were sought. At the suggestion of the United States, a group parallel to the Zangger Committee was formed to include France, which was not an NPT party then, and six other nuclear-supplier nations. Known then as the London Club, it recommended restraint regarding transfers of dual-use items such as enrichment and reprocessing technology, full-scope safeguards and a prohibition against retransfer of nuclear exports to third parties.

Today, the London Club, formally known as the NSG, consists of 28 industrialized countries. In March 1991, after Iraq's procurement activities again raised concerns about the efficacy of nuclear-export controls, the NSG met to update its list of regulated items. In April 1992, the NSG agreed on new guidelines for transferring a wider range of nuclear-related dual-use materials, equipment and technologies, and for reporting such transfers to the IAEA. The NSG compiled a list of 67 dual-use categories of items, all of which are key to producing fissile materials, or nuclear weapons, but also have legitimate civilian uses. NSG members agree to require recipient states to accept full-scope IAEA safeguards.

● *The U.S. Congress:* When it passed the Nuclear Non-Proliferation Act of 1978 (NNPA), Congress underscored IAEA safeguards. Among the provisions of this domestic complement to U.S. nonproliferation efforts, Title II committed the United States to "continued strong support for the principles of the NPT, to a strengthened and more effective IAEA, and to a comprehensive safeguards system administered by the agency to deter proliferation." The NNPA required "full-scope safeguards" on *all* nuclear activities (not just those declared) in nonnuclear-weapons states as a prerequisite for exporting American nuclear technology. When first proposed, this provision proved controversial because it was applied retroactively and unilaterally. Over time, however, the NNPA has gained acceptance as setting a standard for nuclear exports.

After the breakup of the Soviet Union in 1991, Congress funded initiatives to ensure that Soviet nuclear weapons were dismantled. Russia, Belarus, Ukraine and Kazakhstan possessed Soviet strategic and tactical nuclear weapons on their territories, but Russia, as the sole nuclear-weapons successor-state to the Soviet Union, maintained control over them. The Soviet Threat Reduction Act became law in November 1991. Sponsored by Senators Sam Nunn (D-Ga.) and Richard G. Lugar (R-Ind.), this and subsequent legislation, commonly referred to as the Nunn-Lugar Act, have become central to U.S. efforts to denuclearize the former Soviet Union.

The Nunn-Lugar Act initially authorized the Defense Department to transfer up to $400 million to the former Soviet Union to (1) destroy nuclear weapons, chemical weapons and other arms; (2) transport, store, disable and safeguard weapons in connection with their destruction; and (3) establish verifiable safeguards against the proliferation of such weapons. Additionally, more funds have been sought for environmental cleanup of military bases and conversion of defense industries. The fiscal year (FY) 1994 Defense Authorization Act raised the amount to $1.2 billion, and President Clinton requested an additional $400 million for FY 1995. Because of difficulties in negotiations on implementing agreements with Russia, Ukraine, Kazakhstan and Belarus, and in meeting U.S. procedural budgeting requirements, actual expenditure of the funds has been very slow. From November 1991 to July 1994, only 5 percent of the funds had been spent; the Pentagon has been charged to seek ways to streamline this process.

Nuclear Hot Spots

On the morning of December 25, 1991, Soviet President Mikhail S. Gorbachev left his dacha in the woods outside Moscow and climbed into his Zil limousine for his last trip to the Kremlin as President of the U.S.S.R. When he arrived, the presidential nameplate had been changed to "Yeltsin, Boris Nikolayevich." The Russian tricolor flag now flew over the Kremlin instead of the red and yellow hammer and sickle, a clear sign that Soviet rule and the Soviet empire had come to an end. This changing of the guard also represented much more than an epilogue for the Soviet Union; it promised the cessation of a nuclear competition that had spanned more than four decades. On February 1, 1992, at Camp David, Md., President George Bush proclaimed "the end of the cold war and the dawn of a new era." Yeltsin, standing alongside Bush, agreed: "From now on, we do not consider ourselves...enemies."

The end of the cold war affords unprecedented opportu-

nities for cooperation, options that would have been un-
thinkable a decade ago. Significant cuts in both military bud-
gets and force structures are under way, and further reduction of nuclear and conventional arsenals looks promising.
Many Americans are enthusiastic about cashing in on a
"peace dividend," with resources once spent on the superpower competition now being applied to nonmilitary needs.

While there is a sound basis for optimism, it is tempered
by the fact that the end of the cold war and the Soviet
breakup have ushered in new dangers. Although most military analysts agree that the nuclear threat has been greatly
reduced and more force reductions are likely, they are less
certain about the longer-term status of nuclear and conventional arms. Their worries focus primarily on Russia, which
retains a very large nuclear arsenal and whose political future is uncertain.

As for the proliferation threat, the disintegration of the
U.S.S.R. prompted two particular concerns: one was that
Ukraine or other successor-republics would seek to become
new nuclear-weapons states; the second was that Russia and
other successor-states might illegally export Soviet nuclear
materials, technology and know-how.

New Nuclear-Weapons States?

It is possible that the successor-states to the Soviet Union
will reduce their military forces and join in supporting the
nuclear nonproliferation regime. American efforts have thus
far encouraged such a path. The United States has endeav-
ored to keep Soviet nuclear weapons under the control of
Russia and has encouraged nonnuclear successor-states to
sign the NPT. In May 1992, Belarus, Kazakhstan and
Ukraine agreed in the Lisbon protocols to the Start I Treaty
to return all Soviet nuclear weapons on their territory to Russia. They also agreed to sign the NPT "as soon as possible."
By late 1993, Belarus and Kazakhstan had signed, but
Ukraine, a country of 52 million people, and the world's
third-largest nuclear-weapons power, caused considerable

concern, since clearly it was in no rush to accept the treaty.

The United States feared that Ukraine might wish to assert and protect its sovereignty by retaining some nuclear weapons. Although Ukraine has been transferring to Russia a large number of nuclear weapons that had been deployed on its territory, some Ukrainian leaders wanted to retain a number of warheads as a hedge against potential Russian ambitions.

University of Chicago professor John J. Mearsheimer has supported the notion of a Ukrainian nuclear deterrent. Since Ukraine has a history of bad relations with Russia, and those relations are not likely to improve, he believes Ukraine can neither expect to defend itself against a nuclear-armed Russia nor anticipate any meaningful security guarantees from the West (including the United States). Consequently, "Ukrainian nuclear weapons are the only reliable deterrent to Russian aggression," and they will bring a true measure of stability to the region. There is one major problem, Mearsheimer admits: Russia continues to control the existing nuclear arms in Ukraine.

Harvard University professor Steven E. Miller has taken issue with Mearsheimer's line of argument. Miller contends that Mearsheimer is applying cold-war logic to a post-cold-war world, one in which Ukraine finds itself at a distinct disadvantage. "The risks for Ukraine of initiating a nuclear exchange," Miller warns, "will be so great that its deterrent threats will lack credibility." Moreover, the costs of developing a Ukrainian nuclear deterrent, both financial and diplomatic, he asserts, far outweigh the potential benefits. Given Ukraine's moribund economy, it can neither afford to build and maintain nuclear weapons nor alienate the nonproliferation-minded Western democracies from which it seeks economic aid. Furthermore, Ukraine cannot flip a switch to make nuclear weapons; it would have to commit to a long-term program that in the interim would render the nation very vulnerable.

The Clinton Administration pressed Ukraine to honor its

Cartoonists & Writers Syndicate
Palma, *Expresso*, Lisbon, Portugal

agreement under Start I to transfer its nuclear weapons to Russia and sign the NPT as a non-weapons state. On January 14, 1994, President Clinton, Russian President Yeltsin and then President Leonid M. Kravchuk of Ukraine met in Moscow to resolve the impasse of Ukrainian denu-clearization. The three leaders came to an understand-ing, spelled out in a trilateral declara-tion, that provided a number of "car-rots" for Ukraine in exchange for its re-affirmation of a commitment to a nonnuclear status.

First, Russia will provide Ukraine with nuclear fuel elements to keep its electric power plants operating in exchange for the enriched uranium in the warheads that Ukraine has returned to Russia; all nuclear weapons on Ukrainian territory will be out in three years. Second, Washington, for its part, agreed to pay Russia up front for the dismantlement of the warheads, fabrication of fuel elements, and for enriched uranium that it will sell to the United States.

Ukraine's parliament ratified Start I unconditionally in February 1994. And in November, on the eve of a visit to the

U.S. by Leonid D. Kuchma, Ukraine's newly elected president, the parliament voted overwhelmingly to ratify the NPT. One of the few conditions was that Russia, the United States and Britain would respect Ukraine's borders and never use nuclear weapons against it. Parliament's agreement cleared the way for Russia to implement Start I and for the Russian parliament and the U.S. Congress to ratify Start II.

Post-Soviet 'Nuclear Yard Sales'?

Most experts believe that nuclear exports from the former Soviet Union constitute a grave risk. With deteriorating economies, declining defense spending, widespread job insecurity, a need for hard currency, and a surplus of nuclear materials and expertise, the incentives for successor-states to sell abroad have proved compelling. It is estimated that 170 tons of weapons-grade plutonium and 1,000 tons of highly enriched uranium have been produced by the Soviet nuclear-weapons program over the last 40 years. In addition, unknown amounts of plutonium have been separated from civilian nuclear-reactor wastes.

Some individuals have tried to smuggle nuclear-weapons technology and materials out of the former U.S.S.R. In one case, soldiers looking for illegal drugs at a Russian roadblock instead reportedly found nuclear-weapons components stolen from a former Soviet nuclear laboratory. In Germany, from May to August 1994, four arrests of nuclear smugglers, allegedly concealing weapons-grade plutonium and uranium, heightened concern about a nuclear black market originating in the former Soviet Union.

Beyond pressing successor-states to sign the NPT, the United States has tried to stop "nuclear yard sales" by promoting nuclear-export controls and preventing a post-Soviet "nuclear brain drain." President Bush took the first initiatives, which have also been adopted as priorities by the Clinton Administration. In response to U.S. pressure, President Yeltsin agreed to establish nuclear-export-control laws in Russia; at the September 1994 summit in Washington,

D.C., Presidents Yeltsin and Clinton agreed to train Russian border guards to better detect nuclear smugglers. To stem the brain drain, under Nunn-Lugar funding President Bush originally pledged $25 million toward establishing an International Science and Technology Center in Moscow and another $10 million for a branch in Kiev. Thus far, 54 research projects have been approved to employ former nuclear scientists and engineers in areas such as biotechnology, medicine, nuclear-reactor safety and radioactive-waste management. Current plans call for sponsoring 3,000 scientists for about three years.

The planned dismantlement of thousands of nuclear warheads under the Start I and Start II accords, which call for lowering the number of strategic warheads in the United States and former Soviet Union to between 3,000 and 3,500, will add large amounts of weapons-grade materials to the existing stockpiles. Experts have advocated placing all these materials under IAEA safeguards, but this may prove difficult because the agency has had limited resources and increasing responsibilities since the end of the cold war.

Other Nuclear Proliferation Hot Spots

Just as in the former Soviet Union, the nonproliferation outlook elsewhere in the world is somewhat mixed. On the positive side, Argentina and Brazil, once suspected of harboring nuclear ambitions, have negotiated a joint safeguards agreement with the IAEA. Both countries have also signed the Treaty of Tlatelolco. Argentina has joined the Nuclear Suppliers Group, and is moving toward signing the NPT. South Africa joined the NPT in 1991 after it dismantled its six nuclear weapons and has opened its nuclear facilities to IAEA inspection. China and France, two nuclear-weapons-state holdouts, joined the NPT in 1992. And finally, the Nuclear Suppliers Group has tightened export controls.

On the negative side, however, the emergence of an international system with more than two centers of power has increased insecurity in some regions and has induced certain nations to consider (or reconsider) the nuclear-weapons option. Beyond the worries already mentioned about the former Soviet Union, three additional regions remain of particular concern: Northeast Asia (specifically, North Korea), the Middle East (Iraq, Iran and Israel), and South Asia (India and Pakistan). North Korea, Iraq and Iran are parties to the NPT as nonnuclear-weapons states. Israel, India and Pakistan, however, are not parties to the NPT but allow some IAEA inspections. In each of these regions, significant proliferation problems will test the mettle of the post-cold-war nuclear nonproliferation regime.

Northeast Asia: North Korea

North Korea signed the NPT in 1985, but did not permit IAEA inspections until 1992. On April 9, 1992, the North Korean parliament ratified the IAEA safeguards pact, "on condition that any country which joined the NPT will not deploy nuclear weapons on the Korean peninsula nor present a nuclear threat to us." When IAEA inspectors arrived, they found discrepancies in North Korea's initial declaration of nuclear material; samples taken by inspectors showed that North Korea had produced more plutonium than it had acknowledged. Moreover, inspectors were prevented from conducting some crucial tests needed to verify that no nuclear materials had been diverted from seven declared nuclear sites.

Then in February 1993, North Korea denied IAEA inspectors access to two additional undeclared sites suspected of storing nuclear-waste products. The IAEA reasserted its right to search these facilities and requested a special inspection. On March 12, complaining that the IAEA's demands violated its national sovereignty, North Korea began the three-month process of withdrawing from the NPT. On April 1, 1993, the IAEA Board of Governors informed the UN Security Council that North Korea was in noncompliance with the NPT. On May 11, the Security Council passed a resolution that urged North Korea to revoke its withdrawal from the NPT and to allow inspections of the facilities in question; North Korea rejected both requests.

In June 1993, North Korea put its withdrawal on hold, raising issues about the country's legal status under the treaty, and it announced it would no longer allow inspections of its declared facilities. In effect, the North Koreans had jeopardized the continuity of IAEA safeguards. Also in June, the first round of talks between the United States and North Korea to try to break the impasse took place in New York City. By November, however, IAEA Director General Hans Blix warned that his organization could no longer ensure that North Korea's declared nuclear materials were used solely for peaceful purposes. By December, U.S. intelligence agencies estimated a better-than-even probability that North Korea had enough nuclear material for one weapon.

In March 1994, after a second round of talks, North Korea readmitted inspectors to visit the seven declared sites (but not the two undeclared ones). Worrisome evidence sprang from the inspection of the seventh site at Yongbyon (what North Korea calls a "radiochemical laboratory"), a nuclear complex suspected of being a reprocessing plant for extracting plutonium from nuclear spent fuel.* Seals put on an area containing a glove box during an earlier IAEA visit had been broken; "a janitor's mistake," explained the North Koreans. But then the inspectors were not allowed to take samples from the glove box to verify either the janitorial fumble or that the plutonium stocks had been properly handled. In March, the IAEA Board of Governors passed another resolution finding North Korea in noncompliance.

North Korean rhetoric intensified as the specter of international sanctions loomed large: "sanctions would amount to an act of war," the North Koreans warned. In talks with the South Koreans, one North Korean diplomat threatened to turn their capital city, Seoul, into a "sea of flames," should war break out. And unlike the desert war fought against Iraq, a second Korean war would begin just 30 miles from the seat of government and economic center of America's key ally in the region. Two thirds of North Korea's army of 1 million soldiers is deployed within 100 miles of Seoul. General Gary E. Luck, the commander of 37,000 American troops stationed in South Korea, commenting on North Korea, has said, "the place is going to implode or explode. I hope it's an implosion. Because I don't think the world would like to see what an explosion looks like."

The key issue then as now involved convincing North Korea to live up to its NPT obligations. If this failed, the wrong message would be sent to other nuclear aspirants and might even incite regional arms races. "A few nuclear weapons in North Korea," said former Defense Secretary Harold Brown (1977–81), "could have a significant effect on the possibility of nuclear programs in Japan, South Korea and Taiwan." Moreover, regardless of whether it had the bomb, North Korea could sell nuclear technology or materials elsewhere, for example, to Iran. Former Central Intelligence Agency (CIA) director R. James Woolsey accused North Korea of building missiles that could reach Japan and selling missiles to countries in the Middle East.

In its negotiations, the Clinton Administration used "carrots and sticks," betting that the North Koreans could be persuaded to trade away their bombs—or at least their capacity to build them—in exchange for diplomatic recognition and economic assistance. Some argued, however, that these incentives probably meant little to the leaders of an isolated country who remain aloof to world opinion, no matter what the economic consequences. By continuing to negotiate, they said, the United States risked elevating still further the value of the North Korean nuclear card. Kim Il Sung, the North Korean Communist dictator who had ruled since 1948, was undoubtedly testing a theory that says nothing makes Washington take you seriously faster than a pile of plutonium.

In April 1994 a new crisis loomed. North Korea notified the IAEA that it planned to unload some 8,000 fuel rods from its five-megawatt nuclear reactor in Yongbyon without IAEA

Former President Jimmy Carter crosses the demarcation line between the two Koreas as he returns from a 'private' peace mission to the North, June 18, 1994.

Reuters/Bettmann

supervision. Secretary of Defense Perry believes that the fuel rods from this reactor contained enough plutonium to build four or five nuclear weapons. By May, South Korean President Kim Young Sam said that his government had run out of patience and that North Korea's nuclear development should be blocked. By mid-June, as the United States pressed for UN sanctions, South Korea called up over a million reserves for duty. Washington dispatched 48 Patriot missiles to South Korea to protect against possible North Korean missile attacks.

As tensions mounted, former President Carter made a "private" visit to North Korea, seeking ways to reopen negotiations with Kim Il Sung. Carter, critical of U.S. policy in Korea, feared war was imminent. From Pyongyang, the North Korean capital, Carter announced on CNN that he had, after six hours of talks with Kim, reached a "diplomatic breakthrough." North Korea was prepared to allow inspectors back to its installation in Yongbyon if "good faith" bilateral high-level talks with the United States were to be resumed. The death of Kim Il Sung on July 8, 1994, added new uncertainties. Although little was known about Kim Il Sung, even less is known about his son, Kim Jong Il, who has ostensibly succeeded his father.

Talks between the United States and North Korea resumed in August 1994. After two months of intense negotiations, President Clinton, on October 18, approved an agreement calling for more than $4 billion in energy aid to North Korea over the next decade in exchange for a commitment from the North Korean leadership to freeze and gradually dismantle its nuclear-weapons program. A consortium of nations, led by South Korea and Japan, will provide for the construction of two light-water nuclear reactors, designed to make the conversion of nuclear waste into nuclear weapons far more difficult. Under the accord, North Korea must allow full and continuous inspections of its nuclear sites, suspend construction of two new nuclear reactors and then later dismantle some of its key nuclear plants and ship its spent nuclear fuel rods out of the country. Critics of the plan contend that North Korea can keep the spent fuel rods for years, surrendering them only when the new plants are near completion. Based on past experience, they say, North Koreans could also renege on the agreement—as they have before—and reject IAEA inspections.

If North Korea ultimately complies with IAEA demands, the agency's authority and political stature will likely strengthen along with support for the nonproliferation regime; on the other hand, if North Korea is merely veiling its intention to build a bomb, and if the UN Security Council does not insist on unambiguous implementation of nonproliferation commitments, the value of the NPT and the IAEA's safeguards system could be weakened.

The Middle East: Iraq, Iran and Israel

An ongoing challenge faces the nonproliferation regime from Iraq, another NPT signatory with nuclear ambitions. A desire for regional hegemony, as well as fear of Israel's acquisition of the bomb and the threat of renewed conflict with Iran, stimulated Iraq's nuclear program. Iraq, a charter nonnuclear member of the NPT, had one known research reactor subject to IAEA safeguards. Although there was some evidence in the 1980s that Iraq might be attempting to build nuclear weapons, the IAEA did not detect secret uranium-enrichment programs in Iraq prior to its invasion of Kuwait in 1990 and the ensuing Persian Gulf war. It remains an embarrassment to the IAEA that if Iraqi President Saddam Hussein had not invaded Kuwait, he probably would have succeeded in acquiring nuclear weapons.

Inspections by IAEA teams after the Persian Gulf war revealed a large, complex and secret nuclear-weapons project. The Iraqi atomic-bomb project cost several billion dollars and involved thousands of skilled technicians, many of whom were trained in the West. Using oil revenues, Iraq bought equipment and materials that it could not make or purchase through legitimate means from an extensive international network. Saddam Hussein had hoped to produce some weapons-grade uranium by late 1993 and eventually enough to make several nuclear weapons a year.

On April 3, 1991, the UN Security Council authorized the IAEA to conduct inspections anywhere in the country in search of nuclear facilities and to destroy all installations and equipment that could be used to build nuclear weapons. As of September 1994, the IAEA had made 21 inspections. Most of the personnel conducting the inspections have been experts from nuclear-weapons states.

Saddam Hussein threatened or harassed IAEA teams, interfered with helicopter flights, refused inspections and destroyed evidence. After repeated violations of cease-fire and inspection agreements, President Bush ordered U.S. forces to attack sites in Iraq on January 13, 1993, and the assault continued until Iraq agreed to a cease-fire on January 19, 1993.

Ambassador Rolf Ekeus, UN special commissioner for Iraqi disarmament, warned in April 1993 that the Iraqi program would "sprout like a mushroom" as soon as IAEA monitoring ended. On June 29, 1993, at a hearing of the House Foreign Affairs Committee, Assistant Secretary of State Robert L. Gallucci commented that Iraq remained a long-term proliferation threat—a conclusion drawn largely from the experience of the inspection teams. The Iraqi case provided a nuclear wake-up call for the IAEA and, by extension, the nonproliferation regime. Because of the Iraqi and North Korean experiences, the IAEA is considering a number of proposals to strengthen safeguards.

Iran: Seeking a Bomb?

In the 1960s, Shah Mohammad Reza Pahlavi initiated a nuclear-power program that provided Iran with a strong cadre of trained technicians. The shah's widely publicized program, although subject to IAEA safeguards (Iran is an NPT member), may have also accommodated a veiled nuclear-weapons research effort.

The revolutionary government of Ayatollah Ruhollah Khomeini, who took power in 1979, inherited the Tehran Nuclear Research Center, but when it launched its antimodernization programs, the Iranian government temporarily froze nuclear-reactor construction. Many nuclear technicians fled the country. By 1984, however, the Khomeini regime reconsidered its options and opened a new nuclear-research center at Isfahan, former Persian capital.

Iran's defeat by Iraq in 1988, after an eight-year war touched off by a boundary dispute, further rekindled Iranian interest in nuclear research. In October 1988, Hojatolislam Hashemi Rafsanjani, then the commander in chief of Iran's armed forces, openly called for the development of nuclear weapons. After the death of Ayatollah Khomeini in 1989, Rafsanjani was elected president of Iran under a new constitution that granted him expanded powers.

Since then, despite U.S. efforts to embargo nuclear transfers, Tehran may have acquired nuclear assistance from China and North Korea—both major arms suppliers to Iran during the Iran-Iraq war. Furthermore, in September 1991,

Iran tried to purchase a large 30-megawatt nuclear reactor from India that could have produced enough plutonium to make several nuclear weapons annually. India did supply a 10-megawatt reactor, a sale opposed by the United States, but pledged that it would be subject to IAEA safeguards. One Iranian official, quoted in *The New York Times* of October 31, 1991, asserted that Muslim states needed to build nuclear weapons to balance Israel's undeclared nuclear capability. Another, interviewed by a German newspaper, remarked, "We should like to acquire the technical know-how and industrial facilities required to manufacture nuclear weapons, just in case we need them."

In 1992, Iran sought to buy nuclear-reprocessing equipment from Argentina, but the sale fell through due to U.S. pressure. That same year, Russia and China both promised to supply two reactors to Iran under IAEA safeguards, sales also opposed by the United States. Unconfirmed reports that year accused Iran of recruiting Russian nuclear scientists.

Both the Bush and Clinton Administrations have maintained that an Iranian bomb is contrary to U.S. interests, would threaten the other states in the Middle East, possibly derail the Middle East peace process, and spur other states in the region to renew their interest in nuclear weapons. On October 23, 1992, President Bush signed the Iran-Iraq Arms Nonproliferation Act that opposes any transfer of goods or technology to Iraq or Iran that might contribute to either country's acquisition of chemical, biological, nuclear or advanced conventional weapons. In February 1993, then CIA director Woolsey testified before the Senate Government Affairs Committee that "Iran probably will take at least eight to ten years to produce its own nuclear weapons, perhaps sooner if it receives critical foreign assistance."

The Clinton Administration's strategy toward Iran and Iraq is one of "dual containment." Writing in the March/April 1994 issue of *Foreign Affairs,* Anthony Lake, the President's national security adviser, argues that the United States must devise strategies to contain and eventually transform Iran and Iraq: not only do they defy nonproliferation efforts, but they also border the vital Persian Gulf. Containment of Iran, however, is more problematic "because the Administration is not backed by an international consensus reflected in the UN Security Council resolutions, as in Iraq's case." To counter what Lake calls "Iran's quest for domination of the Persian Gulf," he proposes working closely with allies to prevent the transfer of materials and technology that can be used to build weapons of mass destruction.

F. Gregory Gause III, fellow at the Council on Foreign Relations in New York City, takes issue with dual containment, suggesting it is flawed and fraught with dangerous inconsistencies. The most glaring mistake, he argues, "is the contention that Iran and Iraq can be contained simultaneously," because "containment of Iran requires a relatively strong and unified Iraq on its long western border." Gause suggests that a more realistic approach would be for the United States to consult with Iran on the future of Iraq, emphasizing that "the United States does not seek to turn a post-Saddam Iraq into an American asset aimed at increasing Iran's isolation." Isolating Iran economically and strategically, Gause argues, "will provide more impetus for those in Tehran who argue that a nuclear capacity is the only way to hold Iran's enemies at bay."

Existing nuclear suspicions aside, an "Iranian smoking gun" has yet to be found, and the IAEA has reported no unexplained discrepancies in Iran's nuclear materials. Nonetheless, as Zachary Davis and Warren Donnelly, experts at the Congressional Research Service in Washington, D.C., have concluded, "there certainly is enough evidence to call for watchful monitoring, backed by some contingency planning if Iran should move decisively toward nuclear weapons." While Iran continues to assert that all its nuclear activities are for peaceful purposes, some radical political factions clearly favor nuclear weapons. By virtue of this interest, and Iran's location in the volatile Middle East, Iran can expect to remain on the nonproliferation watch list.

Israel: The 'Ambiguous' Arsenal

Israel began its nuclear-weapons program in the mid-1950s, with cooperation from France. Following the Suez crisis of 1956, France and Israel both felt threatened by Arab nationalism, leading France secretly to supply Israel with a plutonium-production reactor (located near Dimona in the Negev desert), weapons design and weapons-manufacture information. Israel bought heavy water, essential for the reactor's operation, from Norway. By 1974, the U.S. CIA reported, "We believe that Israel has already produced nuclear weapons." In 1986, *The Sunday Times* of London published extensive interviews with Mordechai Vanunu, a technician who had worked at Dimona for almost 10 years. Vanunu reported that Israel had produced enough plutonium to make "at least 100 and as many as 200 nuclear weapons of varying destructive power." McGeorge Bundy, in his book *Danger and Survival: Choices about the Bomb in the First Fifty Years,* concluded that Vanunu's testimony "showed that the Israeli program fully justified the designation of Israel as the sixth nuclear power."

Israel, however, has maintained a policy of strict secrecy regarding its nuclear-weapons program. It does not admit to having nuclear weapons, although Israeli officials tacitly imply having the capacity to deploy them as a last resort. It has formally maintained since 1962 that "there are no nuclear weapons in the Middle East and Israel will never be the first to introduce them." This "ambiguity" between the evidence and the Israeli "no bombs" posture is intended to deter enemies in the Middle East from mounting a military attack that might threaten Israel's existence. The U.S. government has accepted this Israeli ambiguity, but in so doing has raised the issue of America playing favorites in its efforts to limit the spread of nuclear weapons. Moreover, for Iraq, and possibly Iran, Israel's undeclared nuclear arsenal has been one of the reasons for rationalizing clandestine nuclear-weapons programs. Israel has not signed the NPT, and is not likely to sign it in the near future.

South Asia: India and Pakistan

India and Pakistan, neither of which has signed the NPT, have gone to war with each other three times since independence in 1947. Insurgents shoot at each other almost on a daily basis in three troubled areas: Kashmir, the Siachan Glacier (northern Kashmir), and Punjab. According to *Arms Control Today,* a publication of the Washington-based nonpartisan Arms Control Association, U.S. intelligence agencies contend that India and Pakistan have all the components necessary to make nuclear weapons, within hours if necessary. In 1993, then CIA director Woolsey warned that this hot spot "poses perhaps the most probable prospect for future use of weapons of mass destruction, including nuclear weapons." The next stage of this regional arms race has already begun; both India and Pakistan are seeking to obtain ballistic missiles that could carry nuclear warheads.

India's motive for developing nuclear weapons stemmed from concerns in the 1960s over the nuclear threat from the PRC, a desire for regional power and world influence, and, since the mid-1980s, a perceived need for keeping ahead of Pakistan's nuclear program. In the 1980s, Prime Minister Indira Gandhi enlarged India's capacity to build nuclear weapons and, despite pressure from the United States, refused to put key facilities under IAEA safeguards. These facilities, which form the backbone of India's nuclear potential, include two nuclear reactors, called Madras I and II; a research reactor at the Bhabha Atomic Research Center near Bombay; a refurbished plutonium-extraction plant at the same site; and a plutonium-extraction plant at Tarapur. While India has not deployed nuclear weapons, it has consistently expanded its capacity to build them.

Pakistan, in the aftermath of war with India in 1971, launched its own nuclear-weapons program. India's test of a "peaceful nuclear device" in 1974 provided additional motivation. By early 1979, the Carter Administration criticized the Pakistanis for their nuclear activities, and Congress passed nonproliferation legislation that led to a cutoff of

American economic and military aid to Pakistan. Later that year, however, with the fall of the shah of Iran and the consequent loss of American listening posts for gathering intelligence about the Soviet Union, President Carter rescinded the cutoff, hoping to relocate the facilities in Pakistan. The Soviet invasion of Afghanistan in December 1979 prompted the United States to suspend temporarily its nonproliferation efforts. American leaders looked to Pakistan to serve as the anti-Communist bulwark in the region.

By the mid-1980s, Pakistan, with Chinese help, had the ability to build a nuclear device. This led Congress to pass the Pressler amendment (named after Senator Larry Pressler, R-S.D.), which linked U.S. bilateral assistance to Pakistan's good nuclear behavior. The U.S. President must certify annually that Pakistan does not possess the capacity to build nuclear weapons before American aid can be authorized. It was not until 1990, after Soviet troops had withdrawn from Afghanistan, that the United States denied all economic and military aid to Pakistan because of its nuclear activities.

As of 1992, Pakistan was believed to have the necessary materials for two nuclear bombs and enough uranium for ten. Pakistani Foreign Minister Shahryar Khan admitted in February of that year that "the capability is there: elements which, if put together, would become a [nuclear] device." India's potential arsenal, experts believe, is much larger, perhaps containing enough components to build between 40 and 60 weapons.

As superpower influence in the region diminished after the cold war, tensions between India and Pakistan worsened, and border disputes in Kashmir threatened to escalate into a nuclear war. Of all the regions where nuclear proliferation is suspected, experts are the most concerned about South Asia. Leonard Spector of the Carnegie Endowment for International Peace in Washington, D.C., said in 1992, "In South Asia we're dealing with an after-the-fact situation. Nuclear weapons have been there for 18 years. It's much harder to roll back nuclear capability than it is to stop it before it is achieved."

Nonetheless, George Perkovich, director of the Secure Society program of the W. Alton Jones Foundation in Charlottesville, Va., still can find a silver lining in the South Asian storm clouds: To date, nuclear war has been averted in the region thanks to what he calls "nonweaponized deterrence." "The fact that neither India nor Pakistan has chosen to build nuclear weapons," he argues, "suggests that near-term policies designed to encourage both sides to refrain from turning know-how into actual weapons could be framed positively—neither country would have to openly surrender anything of value." Knowing that the other can build nuclear weapons quickly, neither India nor Pakistan has chosen to build them. This approach, although admittedly not optimal, Perkovich adds, has worked as a regional form of deterrence. Such an arrangement functions because it was conceived by the two countries with the greatest stake in their own security. Just as the superpowers deterred each other with nuclear weapons, India and Pakistan may choose to deter each other with the *prospect* of nuclear weapons.

The Clinton Administration is worried about the potential failure of deterrence in South Asia—whether it be weaponized or nonweaponized. In April 1994, Deputy Secretary of State Strobe Talbott was dispatched to India and Pakistan to negotiate a cap on their nuclear-weapons and ballistic-missiles race. His proposals, which largely fell on deaf ears, involved permitting Pakistan to take possession of 38 F-16 fighters, on order from the United States since the late 1980s and paid for, in exchange for Pakistan's halting the production of fissile materials, accepting comprehensive safeguards on all its nuclear activities, and refraining from deployment of medium-range missiles purchased from China. A major objective behind capping Pakistani production is to stop the arms race with India. Another concern is that Pakistan might sell highly enriched uranium to neighboring Iran. Pakistani Prime Minister Benazir Bhutto rejected the offer on April 7, saying her country did not want these "useless aircraft if it means that we have to bargain away Pakistan's nuclear program."

Pakistan always looks warily over its shoulder at its nuclear-capable neighbor, India, and does not want its nuclear program singled out as the culprit in South Asia. Since 1990, when President Bush first deemed certification impossible, there have been recurrent rifts between Washington and Islamabad, the Pakistani capital.

Paula Newberg, a professor at Columbia University's School of International and Public Affairs, argues that the Pressler amendment is a harmful law. "By punishing Pakistan but not India, neither country has any incentive to change policies, and both play the nuclear card more forcefully in their domestic politics." Dr. Etel Solingen, a professor at the University of California at Irvine, agrees and has suggested that American policymakers seek to encourage domestic nonproliferation constituencies within South Asia and take them into account when designing nonproliferation strategies. Solingen asserts that at a time of expanding global democratization, when the superpowers debate budgetary priorities and work to reduce their nuclear arsenals, India and Pakistan cannot remain forever isolated and preoccupied with their own competing domestic priorities.

Ending Proliferation:
A Policy Debate

In recent years encouraging developments on the nuclear nonproliferation front have outnumbered disappointments. China and France have signed the NPT. Argentina and Brazil have resolved their nuclear differences and joined the international nonproliferation regime. Prospects for the long-term extension of the NPT are good, although it is unclear whether agreement can be reached to make the treaty indefinite. (See "Issues for the 1995 NPT Extension Conference," pp. 52–53.)

On the other hand, South Africa managed to develop nuclear weapons without the knowledge of the world community; Iraq almost did; and North Korea may be on its way. The motivation to obtain nuclear weapons is still alive and well. Recent attempts to smuggle weapons-grade plutonium out of the former Soviet Union further attest to a market for fissile materials. Moreover, most modern industrial powers with nuclear facilities, including Italy, Sweden, Germany,

President Clinton on October 18, 1994, approved an agreement calling for North Korea to freeze and dismantle its nuclear-weapons program in exchange for energy aid from a consortium of nations. Robert Gallucci, chief U.S. negotiator, and the North Korean first deputy foreign minister sign the pact in Geneva, Switzerland, October 21, 1994.

Japan, South Korea and Taiwan, could, if they decided to, produce nuclear weapons within a few years—some of them within months.

Is further progress in stemming nuclear-weapons proliferation possible? At a minimum, this would require all states with nuclear weapons, including the three undeclared nuclear states of India, Pakistan and Israel, to reduce their holdings to a small residual deterrent under some form of nuclear monitoring. Or is the international nonproliferation regime too flawed to survive, leading to a world of 20 or more nuclear-weapons states competing with one another to maximize their security? The next decade may provide the answer. Success in controlling the spread of nuclear weapons would serve as powerful motivation for improving international cooperation. Failure of this effort would probably lead to further conflict. Most experts agree that the role of the United States will be decisive in determining the outcome.

Issues for the 1995 NPT Extension Conference

In 1995, when the Treaty on the Non-Proliferation of Nuclear Weapons completes its initial 25-year term, a fifth conference must decide "whether the treaty shall continue in force indefinitely, or shall be extended for an additional fixed period or periods." Contrary to some impressions, the treaty does not expire in 1995.

There are currently 170 NPT signatories—165 nonnuclear and 5 nuclear. A simple majority must agree for there to be an indefinite extension of the treaty. About 100 parties to the NPT are from the Nonaligned Movement, composed of developing countries. One of their goals is the "achievement of disarmament," and they have expressed reservations about supporting the extension unless some of their concerns are addressed.

▶ *Discrimination:* Some nonnuclear countries—and undeclared nuclear states like India and Pakistan—criticize the NPT as being discriminatory: it legitimizes nuclear weapons in the hands of a few nations while banning their acquisition by others. Furthermore, IAEA safeguards are obligatory for nonweapons states but not for nuclear-weapons states. NPT critics further contend that the treaty should contain binding provisions for reversing the arms race and curbing both the quantitative and qualitative improvement of nuclear weaponry. They claim the peaceful benefits of atomic energy have been slow in coming to nonweapons states.

▶ *Nuclear Testing:* At the 1990 NPT review conference, Mexico led a group of nations that wanted the nuclear-weapons states to start negotiating a comprehensive test-ban treaty (CTBT) as a precondition for supporting a final conference report on the NPT. An impasse led to adjournment without a final document.

Since 1992, the United States, Britain, France and Russia have suspended nuclear tests. China has conducted three tests, in 1992, 1993 and 1994, and plans to complete its series in 1996. The United States is committed to concluding a comprehensive test ban at the UN Conference on Disarmament in Geneva, Switzerland, "at the earliest possible time."

Most nonproliferation experts believe that if the CTBT could be ready for signature in April 1995, the chances of an indefinite NPT extension would be greatly enhanced. But most observers also think it unlikely—if not impossible—for some 38 member nations of the UN Conference on Disarmament to agree on all the complex questions of scope, timing, verification, enforcement and treaty language by then.

▶ *Positive and Negative Security Assurances:* The United States has pledged not to use nuclear weapons against states that have not acquired such weapons as long as they are not fighting in alliance with any nuclear-weapons state. The United States, Britain and Russia further agreed on such a "negative security assurance" for Ukraine when it joined the NPT in November 1994. Some nations, particularly Egypt and Nigeria, have argued that negative security assurances have lost their meaning in the post-cold-war era. They have demanded a categorical "no-first-use" pledge in exchange for supporting the indefinite extension of the NPT. China favors such a pledge, but the four remaining nuclear-weapons states are cool to the idea.

▶ *Fissile-Materials Cutoff:* As long as nuclear materials— weapons-grade uranium and plutonium—are declared to the IAEA for safeguarding, the NPT does not limit non-nuclear states' production, whether or not the materials are needed for nuclear-power generation. A common complaint against the NPT has been that nuclear-weapons states continue to develop new weapons. Proponents of a global ban on fissile materials assert that it would address this issue. Moreover, a global fissile-materials cutoff could include non-NPT parties such as India, Pakistan and Israel because it would not discriminate between nuclear-haves and nuclear have-nots. Many experts contend that the combined weight of a ban on fissile materials, a comprehensive test-ban treaty and continued reductions in U.S. and Russian arsenals would enhance the chances of nonnuclear countries agreeing to extend the NPT indefinitely.

Clinton Administration Goals

On September 27, 1993, after an eight-month interagency review, President Clinton signed Presidential Decision Directive 13 (PDD-13) that provided the guidelines for his Administration's nonproliferation policy. On the same day, the President delivered a major speech before the UN on U.S. nonproliferation goals. While PDD-13 remains classified, the President's speech, congressional testimony and government documents have made it clear that nuclear nonproliferation has a high priority on the Clinton national security agenda, which is premised on the belief that in the post-cold-war era, the United States must concern itself as much with the prevention of conflict as with its resolution.

A number of policy considerations are shaping the Clinton Administration's approach to proliferation. First, high priority has been placed on initiatives that strengthen existing nonproliferation norms and agreements. Second, the United States has devoted special attention to regions and countries where the dangers of proliferation are particularly acute. Third, the United States will continue to implement domestic-export controls that take into account both nonproliferation objectives and the commercial needs of American exporters. And fourth, the U.S. will update military planning and doctrine to be able to respond if nonproliferation efforts fail. The latter approach is embodied in the Department of Defense counterproliferation* initiative.

Goal 1: Strengthen Existing Nonproliferation Norms and Agreements. The Administration can point to significant nuclear-arms reductions due to the Start I and II treaties, and President Clinton is committed to the earliest possible conclusion of a CTBT and to indefinite extension of the NPT in 1995. In addition, as noted in a White House fact sheet dated September 27, 1993, "We will seek to ensure that the IAEA has the resources needed to implement its vital safeguards responsibilities, and will work to strengthen the IAEA's ability to detect clandestine nuclear activities." Regarding fissile materials, the United States will "seek to eliminate where possible the accumulation of stockpiles of highly enriched uranium or plutonium," and proposes a multilateral treaty or convention banning the production of fissile materials either for nuclear explosives or outside of international safeguards.

Nuclear Testing Policy—The Background: With the 1995 extension conference, among other issues, in mind, the U.S. Congress began to revise policies on nuclear testing. In September 1992, Congress adopted an amendment by Senators Mark O. Hatfield (R-Ore.), George J. Mitchell (D-Me.) and J. James Exon (D-Neb.), known as the Hatfield amendment, to impose limits on U.S. nuclear tests. The Hatfield amendment mandated a moratorium on nuclear testing for an initial nine-month period, then permits 15 tests, and finally bans tests after September 30, 1996 (unless another nation conducts a test). President Bush signed the bill into law in October 1992. Britain, by extension, since it uses the Nevada site to test its nuclear warheads, also announced a moratorium on nuclear testing.

On July 3, 1993, President Clinton declared that he would extend the moratorium at least through September 1994, but if another nation tested a nuclear weapon before then, he would seek congressional approval to conduct nuclear tests. Clinton also promised to explore means of maintaining the U.S. nuclear stockpile without testing. France and Russia endorsed the U.S. position and joined the moratorium. However, after China's October 1993 nuclear test, President Clinton directed the Department of Energy, in accordance with the Hatfield amendment, to take the necessary steps to enable the United States to conduct a test should it be deemed necessary.

While President Clinton had held that testing would bolster confidence in the safety and reliability of the U.S. nuclear stockpile, he decided ultimately that the political costs of testing outweighed the technical benefits: "A worldwide moratorium would put us in the best position to secure NPT extension." On March 15, 1994, the President announced the U.S. moratorium on nuclear testing would be extended until September 1995. He also committed the United States to renewed negotiations on a CTBT.

Policy Debate: Do the benefits of renewed testing outweigh long-term nonproliferation goals, particularly those set for the 1995 NPT extension conference? Robert Bell, National Security Council senior director for arms control and defense policy, described the deliberations within the Administration: "The debate was whether resumed testing would cripple the chances of meeting U.S. objectives in the review conference....One could argue that there should be no link between the NPT and a comprehensive test ban; that the United States has made great progress in arms control, including great steps under Start I and II to reduce our nuclear arsenal; and that those steps should meet the world's requirements for an indefinite extension of the NPT." "The reality," Bell concluded, "is that extending the moratorium on testing appears to be necessary, though not a sufficient condition for securing NPT extension. Resumed testing would also complicate negotiations on a CTBT. Finally, many bilateral considerations, such as with India, Pakistan, Ukraine and North Korea, would be strengthened by not testing."

Other experts, among them Frank Gaffney, director of the Center for Security Policy, a nonpartisan educational organization in Washington, D.C., disagree with the Clinton policy. "Unfortunately, I believe, Iraq, North Korea, Iran, Syria and others are more apt to regard such unilateral restraint as contemptible weakness by the United States than as a model for them to follow," Gaffney notes. He cites four reasons why responsible nuclear testing promotes U.S. national security: (1) testing ensures the reliability of the national nuclear deterrent; (2) testing improves the safety, security, survivability and effectiveness of the U.S. nuclear arsenal; (3) testing helps in understanding the effects of a nuclear environment on military systems, a prudent measure when others continue to acquire nuclear weapons; and (4) testing assists in comprehending nuclear-weapons design, to avoid technological surprises, allowing the United States to respond to evolving threats.

Fissile-Materials Convention—The Background: A surplus of fissile materials exists as a result of the dismantling of U.S. and Russian nuclear arsenals. A study by the U.S. National Academy of Sciences, *Management and Disposition of Excess Weapons Plutonium,* concludes that the surplus stockpiles are a "clear and present danger to national and international security." The study calls for joint U.S.-Russian action on creating a new regime to halt the production of fissile materials, declaring existing stockpiles, reducing the size of stockpiles, and pursuing strengthened safeguards over all fissile materials worldwide. President Clinton supports the National Academy of Sciences' findings and has taken steps to carry out its recommendations.

The United States has agreed to purchase 500 tons of Russian highly enriched uranium removed from nuclear warheads and convert it to nonweapons-grade uranium. Secretary of Energy Hazel O'Leary considered this initiative "a linchpin in securing the agreement with Ukraine to eliminate its nuclear arsenal." Second, the President has decided to submit all fissile materials "in excess of American defense needs" to inspection by the IAEA, including materials recovered from dismantled nuclear weapons. A "surplus-fissile-material identification and disposition initiative" is under way at the Department of Energy to define the excess fissile materials for future safeguarding. Third, on June 23, 1994, Vice President Al Gore Jr. and Russia's Prime Minister Viktor S. Chernomyrdin agreed to begin phasing out the Russian nuclear reactors that have produced plutonium for weapons purposes (the United States has not produced any plutonium since 1988), contingent on the United States helping Russia develop alternative sources of power for the regions where the reactors are located. And fourth, the Administration supports a fissile-materials-cutoff treaty or convention. Preliminary multilateral discussions have begun, but progress has been slow. At best, negotiations will still be at an early stage when the NPT review conference convenes in April 1995.

Policy Debate: Advocates of a fissile-materials convention consider it critical to halting the nuclear arms race and to the success of nonproliferation. On the other hand, opponents of a fissile-materials cutoff contend that it is at best premature and at worst unwise: since the United States still relies on nuclear weapons for its national security, it would be premature to limit the fissile materials that make a stockpile possible; and with the future of democracy in Russia far from certain—and the possibility of a new ultranationalist like Vladimir Zhirinovsky coming to power—it would be unwise to undercut nuclear deterrence. It may be needed as a hedge against a neo-imperialist Russia.

Other critics of U.S. policy contend that America's buying 500 tons of Russia's highly enriched uranium to convert it to nonweapons-grade uranium does not go far enough: there must be a commitment by both countries to stop production of all highly enriched uranium. Moreover, there is a debate over just how much is exactly "in excess of American defense needs," given the uncertain security environment of the post-cold-war era.

Goal 2: Devote Special Attention to Proliferation Hot Spots. The Administration "will make special efforts to address the proliferation threat in regions of tension such as the Korean peninsula, the Middle East and South Asia, including efforts to address the underlying motivations for weapons acquisition and to promoting regional confidence-building steps." For the Korean peninsula, the U.S. goal remains to achieve a nonnuclear peninsula while making every effort to ensure North Korea's full compliance with its nonproliferation commitments. For the Middle East, parallel to the peace process, the Administration will promote dialogue and confidence-building steps "to create the basis for a Middle East free of weapons of mass destruction." In the Persian Gulf area, the United States will work with other suppliers to contain Iran's nuclear ambitions while preventing the

Iraq tried to hide calutrons, pictured above, used for uranium enrichment, and other parts of its nuclear-weapons program from IAEA inspectors at Falluja, Iraq. The site was eventually discovered.

reconstruction of the Iraqi nuclear-weapons program. In South Asia, the United States will encourage India and Pakistan "to proceed with multilateral discussions of nonproliferation and security issues, with the goal of capping and eventually rolling back their nuclear and missile capabilities." Moreover, the Clinton Administration seeks to intensify efforts to ensure that the former Soviet Union, Eastern Europe and China do not contribute to the spread of weapons of mass destruction and missiles.

Goal 3: Balance Export Controls with U.S. Commercial Needs. For the purpose of strengthening U.S. economic growth, democratization abroad and international stability, the Administration "will review our unilateral dual-use export controls and policies." The object here is to streamline U.S. nonproliferation export controls, review exports on a case-by-case basis, "and not inhibit legitimate exports that play a key role in American economic strength."

Some arms-control advocates have severely criticized this Clinton nonproliferation goal. Gary Milhollin, director of the Wisconsin Project on Nuclear Arms Control, argued in *The Washington Post* that "almost everything needed to make a nuclear weapon is dual-use and current export laws reflect that fact....There is no hope of stopping development of an Iraqi bomb without controlling such exports." Milhollin quoted an unnamed Pentagon expert on clandestine trade who complained that under his boss, Secretary of Defense Perry, "the Pentagon is decontrolling things faster than we can track the ships carrying them." The Clinton Administration, however, sees that export controls must be applied uniformly by all suppliers to be effective and because current U.S. dual-use export controls are more stringent than those of other countries, American exporters have suffered. Moreover, it argues, since American dual-use export controls were designed during the cold war, they need to be reassessed in light of new circumstances.

Goal 4: If Nonproliferation Fails, then Counterproliferation. The Clinton Administration intends to give a higher profile to intelligence collection, analysis and defense planning to "ensure that our own force structure and military planning address the potential threat from weapons of mass destruction." On December 7, 1993, in a speech before the National Academy of Sciences, then Secretary of Defense Les Aspin described a new counterproliferation initiative that is designed to "respond to the nuclear dangers of the new security era, specifically, the danger of proliferation of weapons of mass destruction and the danger posed by the possibility of nuclear spill out from the former Soviet Union."

In a May 1994 *Report on Nonproliferation and Counterproliferation Activities and Programs,* John Deutch, deputy secretary of defense, defined counterproliferation as "the activities of the Department of Defense across the full range of U.S. efforts to combat proliferation, including diplomacy, arms control, export controls, and intelligence collection and analysis, with particular responsibility for assuring U.S. forces and interests can be protected should they confront an adversary armed with weapons of mass destruction." Counterproliferation aims to thwart terrorist groups or rogue nations from acquiring nuclear weapons, and to provide the President with a range of military options in the event that nonproliferation efforts fail. The Department of Defense has budgeted about $400 million for counterproliferation in FY 1995. One option is the theater missile defense system that would include a new mobile antimissile interceptor for use against short- and medium-range missiles, such as those found in North Korea.

Counterproliferation grew out of the experience of the Persian Gulf war, where American soldiers faced the possibility of confronting weapons of mass destruction and where an NPT party (Iraq) had blatantly violated its nonproliferation agreements. Furthermore, heightened tensions with North Korea and concerns about the potential nuclear ambitions of Iran suggested that the Iraqi case may be a harbinger of future confrontations. If nonproliferation treaties need to be enforced, then the United States should prepare for scenarios where American military force might be needed. Proponents of counterproliferation see this strategy as a prudent measure, given the changing nature of the threat to American security.

Critics contend, however, that counterproliferation is an overreaction, perhaps more an effort to secure a role for the defense and intelligence communities in the post-cold-war era and to justify the development of new weapons systems rather than a bona fide national security objective. Moreover, they argue, any preemptive use of force may not only be contrary to international law, it could inflame rather than resolve regional tensions. Serious diplomatic considerations also might come into play. Would the United States be able to count on a UN mandate for preemptive action? What would be the international consequences if it acted unilaterally? And militarily, as in Iraq, it is unclear whether the

United States could destroy all relevant targets that have been dispersed and hidden across wide terrain.

The U.S. Policy Debate

The choice of U.S. policy options regarding nuclear proliferation depends in large part on how one views the role of the United States in the post-cold-war era. With the strategic environment in flux, the United States is adjusting long-standing assumptions regarding nuclear weapons, the threat they pose to U.S. security, and the role they play in assuring it. At issue is the degree to which the United States should step back from, join or lead the efforts to control nuclear proliferation.

Step Back and Close the Nuclear Umbrella: Ted Galen Carpenter, director of Foreign Policy Studies at the Cato Institute, a conservative research organization in Washington, D.C., argues that U.S. leaders should reassess cold-war policies on proliferation and step back from them. "Washington should give up its fruitless obsession with preserving the NPT and the unraveling nonproliferation system that it represents." Harking back to George Washington's Farewell Address (1796), and then catapulting its lessons into the nuclear age, Carpenter warns against "entangling nuclear alliances" that could place the United States at risk in regional nuclear wars that it would have no part in starting nor any interest in fighting. In this context, he views extended deterrence, the cold-war strategy used primarily to link the U.S. nuclear arsenal to the defense of Europe, as no longer relevant. Extended deterrence, Carpenter argues, worked largely because there was no territorial ambiguity in the U.S-Soviet competition. "Both the India-Pakistan and Russia-Ukraine rivalries," he argues, "involve precisely that problem." Moreover, "the North Korea-South Korea confrontation is even more serious; neither regime even accepts the legitimacy of the other."

If proliferation trends continue along these lines, Carpenter worries that the United States might have to deter a number of nuclear states from attacking or intimidating American allies or clients in "a more unwieldy and more dangerous mission than was deterring the U.S.S.R." He concludes that the U.S. nuclear umbrella should be closed now that the cold war is over. The United States can further reduce its arsenal, extend the moratorium on testing and encourage nuclear-free zones, but "the first task of a prudent U.S. security strategy must be to keep America out of the nuclear cross fire."

Strengthen Multilateral Nonproliferation Efforts: This perspective holds that in a more multipolar world, the United States may find it harder to determine the nonproliferation agenda and thus should join other nations in strengthening existing multilateral nonproliferation norms, agreements and initiatives that give the UN a larger role in enforcement. The United States should defer more to multilateral forums such as the IAEA, the UN Conference on Disarmament in Geneva and the UN Security Council.

The U.S. Should Continue to Lead: A third approach calls for the United States neither to withdraw from nor defer, but rather to continue, its global leadership role in nonproliferation. As American power to influence events adjusts to the changing international security environment, the United States, as the remaining superpower, will be looked to for leadership in promoting the international nonproliferation regime and encouraging initiatives that support its goals. A number of ideas have surfaced on how best to lead the international efforts to control the spread of nuclear weapons and obtain an indefinite extension of the NPT.

● The Committee on Non-Proliferation and the Role of the IAEA of the nonprofit Atlantic Council of the United States in Washington, D.C., for example, supports U.S. pressure on the UN Security Council to assert that any violation of NPT commitments to IAEA safeguards will be taken as a threat to international peace and security, and meet with collective response measures under Chapter VII of the UN Charter. It also favors a policy of no-first-use of nuclear weapons.

● Jonathan Dean, arms-control adviser to the Union of Concerned Scientists, a Massachusetts-based advocacy group on nuclear and other issues, would have the United States focus instead on what he calls "the final stage of nuclear arms control," that is, devising a realistic, irreversible "builddown" of nuclear arsenals to fulfill the long-standing disarmament pledges of the NPT. This would include the obligatory dismantling of the number of warheads reduced by negotiation and the handing over of their fissile materials to bilateral or multilateral supervision, and separating nuclear warheads still deployed in the field from their delivery systems and placing both under multilateral monitoring.

● In their book, *Reducing Nuclear Danger: The Road Away from the Brink,* McGeorge Bundy, William J. Crowe Jr. (former chairman of the joint chiefs of staff) and Sidney D. Drell (physicist and professor at Stanford University) warn that "it is not at all clear that the overall *level* of nuclear danger has gone down." The three former government officials blast the nuclear age's "habit of secrecy" and the public's "unjustified belief that only experts with access to secrets could understand these matters."

The authors conclude that "it is time to replace the inherited distinction between those countries with nuclear weapons and those without by a wider assertion that all nations should be on the same side—*against* nuclear danger—whatever their present degree of reliance on nuclear weapons."

Since the dawn of nuclear proliferation in the deserts of New Mexico in 1945, nuclear weapons have posed unprecedented dilemmas for policymakers and their constituencies. Since the end of the cold war, this has not changed. The destructive power of nuclear weapons still attracts those who would seek to have them to protect their national interests, still deters those who might attack potential enemies who possess them, and still horrifies those who fear they will be used in either anger or accident. What has changed, however, is that the opportunity for winning the third nuclear race, of preventing nuclear war by stemming nuclear proliferation, has a reasonable chance of succeeding. And that, after all, is one of the most important post-cold-war challenges.

GLOSSARY

atomic bomb (A-bomb): Bomb whose explosive power comes from the fissionable (see below) nuclei of the isotopes uranium-235 and plutonium-239. The first, tested on July 16, 1945, at Alamogordo, N. Mex., was made with plutonium-239 and carried a force of 17 kilotons of TNT.

counterproliferation: The full range of Defense Department activities to combat nuclear proliferation, including diplomacy, arms control, export controls and intelligence collection and analysis. If nonproliferation efforts fail, it provides military options.

fission: The splitting of uranium or plutonium atomic nuclei into fragments, a process that releases energy in the form of heat, blast and radiation. The process used in atomic bombs.

fusion: The compression of lightweight atomic nuclei into a nucleus of heavier mass, with the attendant release of energy, a process similar to that which occurs in the sun. The process used in hydrogen bombs.

highly enriched uranium: Uranium in which the percentage of uranium-235 nuclei has been increased from the natural level of 0.7 percent to a greater level, usually around 90 percent. Along with plutonium (see below), one of the two fuels essential for making nuclear weapons.

hydrogen bomb (H-bomb, or thermonuclear bomb): Bomb whose explosive power derives largely from nuclear fusion (see above). The first one tested by the United States was nearly 600 times more powerful than the atomic bomb dropped on Hiroshima. Hydrogen bombs have been tested several times but never used in warfare.

Intermediate Nuclear Force Treaty (INF): A 1987 bilateral treaty between the United States and the U.S.S.R. eliminating an entire class of weapons—missiles with a range of 300–3,400 miles.

International Atomic Energy Agency (IAEA): Established in 1957, it has a working relationship with the UN. Under the NPT (see below), parties possessing no nuclear weapons must conclude safeguards agreements with the IAEA, whose main job is to verify that nuclear materials used for energy production in member countries are not diverted to military purposes.

nuclear nonproliferation regime: See **Treaty on the Non-Proliferation of Nuclear Weapons**

plutonium: An isotope which is manufactured artificially when uranium-238, through irradiation, captures an extra neutron. One of the two core materials used in nuclear weapons, the other being highly enriched uranium (see above).

safeguards: System used by the IAEA (see above) to inspect a nation's nuclear facilities that are declared as a result of the country becoming party to the NPT (see below), or as a result of a bilateral agreement. Inspections make use of a mix of material accountancy, containment and surveillance to provide evidence of unauthorized use or transfer of safeguarded nuclear materials.

spent fuel: Nuclear fuel that has been used in a reactor and removed because it contains too little fissile material to sustain reactor operation. Extremely radioactive.

Strategic Arms Limitation Talks (SALT) I: Series of talks from 1969 to 1972 in which the United States and the U.S.S.R. negotiated the first agreements limiting some of their most important armaments. The **Antiballistic Missile Treaty (ABM)** of 1972, amended in 1974, limits ABM systems to a single deployment area of 100 ABM launchers and missiles. In the **Interim Agreement** of 1972, the United States and the U.S.S.R. froze the number of strategic-ballistic-missile launchers at current levels.

Strategic Arms Limitation Talks (SALT) II: Second round of talks, from 1972 to 1979, which ended in agreement by the United States and the U.S.S.R. to set equal aggregate ceilings and subceilings on strategic-offensive-weapons systems and impose restraints on existing and future strategic systems. The agreement was never ratified. The United States repudiated its commitment to remain within the SALT II limits in 1986 in response to alleged Soviet violations.

Strategic Arms Reduction Treaty (Start) I and II: Signed by the United States and the U.S.S.R. in July 1991, Start I provides for the reduction of approximately one third of the strategic warheads of both parties, limiting nuclear warheads to 6,000. Under Start II, signed in January 1993 but not yet ratified, the United States and Russia will reduce strategic warheads to between 3,000 and 3,500 and eliminate land-based missiles with multiple warheads.

Treaty on the Non-Proliferation of Nuclear Weapons (NPT): The cornerstone of the **nuclear nonproliferation regime,** a collection of international efforts to stop the further proliferation of nuclear weapons. A multilateral treaty that entered into force on March 5, 1970, it currently has 170 parties, including the five nuclear-weapons states. In April 1995, an extension conference will decide whether the treaty shall continue in force indefinitely or for an additional fixed period or periods.

weapons of mass destruction (WMD): Nuclear, biological and chemical weapons.

Talking It Over

A Note for Students and Discussion Groups

This issue of the HEADLINE SERIES, like its predecessors, is published for every serious reader, specialized or not, who takes an interest in the subject. Many of our readers will be in classrooms, seminars or community discussion groups. Particularly with them in mind, we present below some discussion questions—suggested as a starting point only—and references for further reading.

Discussion Questions

On September 27, 1993, before the UN, President Clinton outlined the importance of the nuclear proliferation challenge for U.S. interests. Why should the United States care about this issue? To what degree must the United States take a leadership role in nonproliferation? To what degree should it defer to others?

Why do nations build nuclear arsenals in the first place? In each of the three nuclear races in this century, what prompted the nations involved to build the bomb? Is it possible to prevent nuclear proliferation if a nation decides it is in its best interests to "go nuclear"?

What forces have contributed to thwarting nuclear arms-control efforts? What are the lessons of the Cuban missile crisis for nations seeking their own nuclear-weapons capability? What are the components of the nuclear nonproliferation regime? What, in your view, are its strongest and weakest elements? Which, if any, should be strengthened or given more attention? While attention is often focused on the breakdown of the regime, what are its success stories?

The end of the cold war and the breakup of the Soviet Union have brought new nuclear proliferation challenges. What are they, and who can best deal with them? What are the benefits and the drawbacks of the UN taking the leading role?

Has the end of the cold war brought more or less security to the world? Has the great East-West confrontation merely been replaced by smaller regional confrontations? Do you think the post-cold-war crises in Iraq and North Korea show the urgent need for immediate comprehensive nonproliferation efforts? In what ways is that goal clearly reflected in U.S. policy?

Annotated Reading List

Bailey, Kathleen C., *Strengthening Nuclear Non-Proliferation*. Boulder, Colo., Westview Press, 1993. Former Reagan official assesses current U.S. policy options for strengthening the nuclear nonproliferation regime.

Bethe, Hans A., Gottfried, Kurt, and McNamara, Robert S., "The Nuclear Threat: A Proposal." *The New York Review of Books,* June 27, 1991. The authors suggest reducing U.S. and Russian nuclear forces to approximately 5 percent of their current level.

Blix, Hans, "Verification of Nuclear Nonproliferation: The Lesson of Iraq." *The Washington Quarterly,* Autumn 1992. Details lesson learned as a result of Iraq's clandestine program to build a bomb; insightful for understanding subsequent UN and IAEA actions regarding North Korea.

Bundy, McGeorge, Crowe, Jr., William J., and Drell, Sidney D., *Reducing Nuclear Danger: The Road Away from the Brink.* New York, Council on

Foreign Relations, 1993. Three experts offer their prescription for preventing nuclear proliferation and advocate drastically reducing U.S. and Russian arsenals.

Carpenter, Ted Galen, "Life After Proliferation: Closing the Nuclear Umbrella." *Foreign Affairs*, March/April 1994. Carpenter argues that the United States must withdraw from "entangling nuclear alliances."

Clinton, Bill, "Address by the President to the 48th Session of the United Nations General Assembly." *U.S. Department of State Dispatch*, September 27, 1993. Outlines the Clinton Administration's approach to nuclear proliferation.

Dean, Jonathan, "The Final Stage of Nuclear Arms Control." *The Washington Quarterly*, Autumn 1994. Former arms-control negotiator advocates an irreversible "builddown" of nuclear arsenals.

Dunn, Lewis A., "Rethinking the Nuclear Equation: The United States and the New Nuclear Powers." *The Washington Quarterly*, Winter 1994. Clearly describes the changed nature of the nuclear threat and how the United States should rethink its policy to counter it.

Kratzer, Myron B., *International Nuclear Safeguards: Promise and Performance*. Washington, D.C., The Atlantic Council of the United States, April 1994. A cogent and compelling overview of nonproliferation safeguards.

Mack, Andrew, "North Korea and the Bomb." *Foreign Policy*, Summer 1991. Why North Korea wants a nuclear capability and the problems this poses for the nonproliferation regime.

Mearsheimer, John J., "The Case for a Ukrainian Nuclear Deterrent." *Foreign Affairs*, Summer 1993. The author argues that if Ukraine is forced to hedge against Russian expansion by hosting a large conventional army, the risk of war would be much greater than if it had a nuclear arsenal.

Miller, Steven E., "The Case Against a Ukrainian Nuclear Deterrent." *Foreign Affairs*, Summer 1993. In the uncertain environment of the former Soviet Union, the author argues that allowing Ukraine to keep nuclear weapons would be highly dangerous.

Perkovich, George, "A Nuclear Third Way in South Asia." *Foreign Policy*, Summer 1993. The author advocates "nonweaponized deterrence" for dealing with India and Pakistan as an alternative to the traditional NPT-centered approach.

Potter, William C., "Exports and Experts: Proliferation Risks from the New Commonwealth." *Arms Control Today*, January/February 1992. The author explores the proliferation risks stemming from the former Soviet Union, including the flight of nuclear scientists and the spread of weapons-grade materials.

Sokolski, Henry, "Fighting Proliferation with Intelligence." *Orbis*, Spring

1994. Former Defense Department deputy for nonproliferation policy (1989–93) delineates how the government will have to "match U.S. strengths against an adversary's weaknesses in an effort to force it into less-threatening areas of competition."

Solarz, Stephen J., "Next of Kim: How to Stop the North Korean Bomb." *The New Republic,* August 8, 1994. Calls for a hardheaded analysis that takes into account North Korea's continuing nuclear cap

"Special ⟨obscured⟩ es on the Ira⟨obscured⟩

Specto ⟨obscured⟩ *Weapons:* ⟨obscured⟩ Carnegie ⟨obscured⟩ a classic